GEMINI

2005

HINKLER
BOOKS

Cover Design: Sam Grimmer

Published in 2004 by Hinkler Books Pty Ltd
17–23 Redwood Drive
Dingley VIC 3172 Australia
www.hinklerbooks.com

ISBN 1 7412 1555 2
Printed and bound in Australia

CONTENTS

INTRODUCTION

Welcome to the astonishing, intriguing world of horoscopes in astrology. The year 2005 promises to be exciting across all the signs. I hope to navigate you safely through the coming months with some words of wisdom and insight. Consider this little book a road map to a successful and fulfilling year!

Consulting 'the stars' when making decisions is a time-honoured tradition. The American Indians, the South American Inca, the Australian Aborigines and many ancient cultures have looked up into the night sky and given meaning to the turnings of the great astral wheels above them.

Astrology is a science of observation. That is, it is a process developed over thousands of years of observations of the stars and the influence their placement has over all manner of earthly phenomena. Police have observed that a full moon will mean a busy night at the police station. Gardeners have observed that it is better to tend certain vegetables at certain phases of the moon. And meteorologists have observed that longer weather patterns, such as El Nino, can be predicted by the stars.

This guide to your daily horoscopes for 2005 is an extension of that tradition. By looking at the night sky and taking your sun sign into account, it is possible to make predictions about what sort of a year 2005 will be for you.

Part 1 of this book provides a brief history of astrology. I also explain how I made the predictions contained in the day-by-day guide in the second part of the book.

Part 2 gives you the day-by-day guide to the year, with an overview covering the main things that will happen to you in the important areas of relationships, career and money, and health.

Part 3 of the book provides a comprehensive outline of the characteristics of the Gemini sun sign and a full list of your compatibilities with other sun signs.

I wish you the very best in 2005 and hope this book plays some part in your coming successes.

HISTORY

Most historians and astrologers agree that astrology can be traced back to Babylonia (now Iraq) about 3500 years ago, in the first half of the Hammurabi dynasty. The Babylonians, noted for their advanced culture, had a well-developed science of observational astronomy. This provided them with a complex calendar to use for times to plant and harvest, times to hold religious festivals and so on.

Each planet was given importance, and the priests named the planets in honour of their many gods, such as Ishtar, now known as the planet Venus, and Nergal, now known as Mars. By about 1000 BC, the Babylonians had developed a sense of 'planetary omens' and put their minds to setting their system down in literature.

Since Nergal was the god of war, when this planet shone brightly in the sky, the Babylonians took it as a sign that it was a good time to wage war. As Ishtar was the goddess of love, a spring night in which that planet shone high in the west after sunset was considered a good time for romance. This was the first basic horoscope.

It is interesting to note that across the seas in South America, the Incas had also given the same meanings to each planet. This happened even though the two societies grew up independently of each other until the Spanish 'discovered' South America in 1532!

By 600 BC, the Babylonians had devised the twelve-sign zodiac by developing markers in the sky that corresponded roughly to the months of the year. This is when the concept of making predictions based on the signs began to develop and became more complex. Eventually, the Babylonians were able to make a map of the heavens to use in divination.

The oldest horoscope that has been discovered dates to 29 April 410 BC, when it is known that horoscope predictions were extremely popular.

In later centuries, the popularity of astrology waned. By 1900, a French encyclopaedia was describing it as 'a vanishing cult', with 'no young devotees'.

Then came a revival. Astrology bounced back, leading to the remarkable passion and devotion people have for it today. The catalyst was British astrologer RH Naylor who, after World War I, invented the daily newspaper astrology column. It attracted many readers, and now there is barely a newspaper or magazine on the planet that does not publish a regular horoscope.

In these astrological charts, people found a form of self-reflection that they were not finding elsewhere in their lives. The result is that now 90 per cent of all Americans under the age of thirty know their sun sign, and there are more than 10,000 practising astrologers in the United States.

Millions of dollars are spent annually in Australia, the United States and Europe by people consulting astrologers. The Emperor Caligula, Claudius, Ptolemy, St Augustine, Queen Elizabeth I and more recent figures, such as former US president Ronald Reagan and Princess Diana, have all looked to the stars for guidance.

Looks like the Babylonians were on to a good thing!

HOW HOROSCOPES ARE WRITTEN

To come up with your daily horoscope, I have taken the chart of each day (using the Equal House System) and turned the zodiac wheel so that zero degrees of your sign Gemini sits on the ascendant. I take a note of the relationships of your ruling planet (in Gemini's case this is Mercury) and make some rough predictions.

I then look at the planet that rules the sign that Mercury is in at the time of the reading. This planet is called the dispositor, and I make more-detailed assertions from where it sits in relation to Mercury.

When a house contains a lot of planetary energy, this means that aspects of your life will be focussed in that area. I make notes on whether this is easy or difficult energy. Significant events in the heavens, such as when two planets align, are also noted. If a day's energy is particularly significant for your sign, it has been highlighted.

The moon also plays a leading role in any horoscope, so a special note is made of new and full moons.

HOW RELIABLE ARE THEY?

It would be fair to ask at this point, how can we make daily predictions for all the people born in one particular month? Humans are a diverse bunch with different interests and different lifestyles, so how can we categorise people's experiences into only twelve separate boxes?

The problem is in the variables. Each planet, each sign and each house has several different meanings, and it is possible I have chosen the one that is not relevant to you. All the same, the issues are generally similar, so you will get a good idea of how it applies in your situation. As with anything in this world, nothing beats common sense.

There can be no doubting the horoscope's worth in giving people another way to look at a situation, or inspiring them to great things. I hope this book can give you a whole new perspective on a problem that has been troubling you, and provide a framework within which you can look for the meaning in your life.

THE YEAR 2005

YEARLY OVERVIEW

Life is good, is it not Gemini? 2005 promises to let the good times roll on and on. The areas that will be under stress for you are easily laughed off when you consider all the fun and laughter that the universe is providing.

Romantically, you have all the luck in the world right now and this will continue. Geminis are renowned flirts and you will be in your element, wowing them at parties and generally having a wild old time. Your dance card will be perpetually full and you might feel so lucky in love that there won't really be any need to get serious. Don't make that mistake. Luck will leave your romance sector late in the year and switch its attentions to your work sector. Suddenly, life will go back to normal, the merry-go-round will stop and you'll be stuck with whoever you happen to be with at the time. Make sure you've got the right one.

You've not been so lucky when it comes to money and material matters. For a long time now, it has seemed like you couldn't hold on to anything for very long. It might appear like you've developed an easy come, easy go sort of an attitude, but the truth is that the universe is teaching you a lesson about what is important and what is superfluous.

Fortunately, it will have finished its lecturing in mid-July and will have moved its attentions to other areas of your life. If you have been a good student, you will find that issues around your finances become a lot less stressful.

RELATIONSHIPS

This is an exciting and romantic year for you. August and September will be especially full of exotic and intriguing people to meet and talk with as your creativity comes to the fore and you dazzle those around you with your sparkling conversation. You are in your element on the social scene at this time, and you find that loving them and leaving them comes effortlessly. Too effortlessly, in fact, and you might wonder whether you actually helped Mr Wonderful with his coat and let him leave.

A momentous event might occur on 5 September. By early November, you will have settled into a rhythm with someone special and will be exploring the wonderful ways that a partnership can develop. This initial phase is also a great time for established couples to renew their commitment to each other and make some decisions about what will shape their relationship over the next year.

CAREER AND MONEY

There are two major times for your career in 2005, occurring from mid-February to late March and from 1 May through to mid-June.

Opportunities will come thick and fast at these times, and it won't be a question of when should you jump but whether you should jump. You might find that some pearls of opportunity clash with others and it's really up to you to decide which path to take. Make your choice from the available evidence and stick with it through thick and thin. A dream on 15 May will point you in the right direction if you are confused about the path to take.

Money will most certainly be a contributing factor to any decision you make, as there is a heavy emphasis on finances all the way through June. Money will also be reasonably plentiful at this time, so don't be afraid to take a carefully calculated risk. You have the energy to make it work even if luck isn't on your side.

HEALTH

There are excellent indications that you have great scope to change bad habits for the better this year. There is solid emphasis on health throughout the last half of the year.

Your key to breaking bad habits will be to make exercise as much a part of your life as you do for having fun, and you'll be on the path to success. Enrol in something that you love to do but never find the time for, such as Latin dancing or windsurfing, and you'll feel a little decadent but get exercise at the same time.

YOUR DAILY GUIDE

Saturday 1 January
You can't view your own actions objectively when a situation sparks a range of emotions in you. While you are usually a very giving person, you can't quite rationalise your benevolence when you seem to get very little in return. Your confusion is not related to the actions of others at all, but rather to a shift in the way you understand the world.

Sunday 2 January
You're not afraid to bend rules when the situation calls for a little flexibility. Those are the attributes of a good leader and you never know who is watching. In love, showering your partner with sexual fantasies and other sweet things becomes a blissful state for both. The emotions run deep and can be rather erotic, but be careful not to discuss sensitive subjects as you could defuse a very nice situation.

Monday 3 January
As the last quarter of the Moon wanes in the sky, last month's project should be coming to completion. Don't get distracted now, especially as you are so close to the end. There is a tight little community of planets in your relationships sector today. Mercury, Venus and Pluto are playing out a little drama for you that could mean a conversation that turns everything on its head.

Tuesday 4 January
With your will strongly focused, you shouldn't have any trouble acquiring wealth, but your family relationships will begin to come under stress. You are disheartened by

material possessions at times, and it is having a negative influence on other aspects of your life. Focussing on money is not a problem for you, so give to charity and get on with things.

Wednesday 5 January

A company you are associated with or work for is suffering from the collective negativity of its employees. There is a whole swag of issues that you need to raise at work, but you are having trouble identifying a person of authority who you can also respect to any degree. Don't fool yourself that you can change the mindset of an organisation with good will alone.

Thursday 6 January

Just when you think things couldn't get much worse, a loved one will be there for you when you need it the most. They will know just what to say to help you put it all into perspective. In the end, what starts out on the wrong foot could really stumble forward into a great afternoon. There will be an opportunity to get to know someone who fascinates you.

Friday 7 January

Just when you thought nobody was looking you made a crucial blunder or two and now you have everyone on your case. There is no reason to stop feeling good about yourself, and you can easily allow the never-ending advice to fade into a distant murmur. Decide whose advice you respect and listen to them.

Saturday 8 January

Sometimes you hit on ideas that feel so right that you can do nothing to avoid following your instincts. In this case, the risk is over-committing to an ambitious dream, but maybe there is just enough fuel in the tank to get to the Moon and back. Certainly don't limit yourself to goals that are so simple that they leave you unsatisfied when the day is done.

Sunday 9 January

Money isn't the number one thing on your mind, but it certainly helps. While you are on the receiving end of some money, this will allow you to relax your financial guard. You know it's not forever, but at least you get a little shuteye. In fact, the reward for being frugal should at least be the opportunity to buy something for yourself or for someone you love.

Monday 10 January

The new Moon brings food for thought. Choose carefully dear Gemini, because whatever you decide to tackle will shape the next month for you. There is a heavy emphasis on your financial sector that could mean that a loan is on the cards. The mood is contemplative, and you will find you are deeply considered right now and in the zone for an air-cleansing exchange.

Tuesday 11 January

You have a false impression of what it is like to be single and you wrongly think that it compares poorly to your current situation. Your magnetism today will have you held in high regard by the opposite sex, but it won't lure you away from phoney monogamy. You should seek to redefine the way you value your relationship, although it would be a shame to completely back out of the current situation when things were really starting to progress emotionally.

Wednesday 12 January

They say a good friend will stab you in the front, but that does not mean that the wound is less mortal. Impress your friends with your thoughtfulness and arrange something for the weekend to celebrate their place in your life. While friends might prove a little too free with joking insults, they are a good source of advice and are perhaps in the best position to tell you what you need to hear.

Thursday 13 January

There is a great challenge ahead of you, and in order to respond successfully you need to exercise a little craziness. While you think you are the sensible one in your relationships, you lose the initiative in arguments. However, even the people who think you're talking nonsense have no choice but to be amused. In you career, your mind is craving intellectual stimulation, and with your conviction in place, you will perform great actions.

Friday 14 January

There is a great deal of respect to be earned from others as someone who does a good job every time. When you give yourself totally to your work, you might impress upon people your worth, but you also run the risk of burning out and making less desirable impressions. You should view the consistency of your efforts as being just as important as how well you do things.

Saturday 15 January

You have a intuitive feel for money matters lately, but this can be thwarted by the green-eyed monster of financial greed. Today you will want to be close to your homage and the possessions it contains, but something will snap you out of this unusual mood and remind you that there is nothing more valuable than your health and your friends.

Sunday 16 January

There is a sense of desperation to bring about changes in the way you express yourself, and this serves your sense of who you are and how you portray your public face. The ladder is beckoning – are you ready to work your way up it? There is added power to your emotions when you are contemplating your ambitions. With these intense feelings, you can learn to express yourself calmly and warmly in this area of your life, rather than letting a rush of emotions go to your head.

Monday 17 January

As the Moon waxes to half in the sky, your efforts regarding your finances should be well under way. Remember, well begun is half-done. Generally you'll be dragged into things that you never volunteered to do. Someone you thought was a friend seems to be growing away from you. You have been wondering why you're left out in the cold on a social level and maybe there are problems that have been festering below the surface.

Tuesday 18 January

You have a strong aura today as a result of meditation or a spiritual experience and it will help to bring your dreams into perspective. You have an opportunity to focus this energy in a number of ways, but it is best used to help those around you. You can make people feel good by complimenting them, or you can defuse heated situations by stepping in and changing the energy flow of the argument.

Wednesday 19 January

There is a tendency towards being non-combative with your colleagues. But you know that there are other ways of dealing with the frustration that comes about from the clashing of multiple egos. You may have to ask for the assistance of others today, especially when your own ego trips you up in your relationship. Let's just say that tact and charm are not your strong points at the moment, so enlist the help of a friend.

Thursday 20 January

The big picture has been highlighted by the Sun for you. This month is a great time to assess the progress of your long-term goals. Are you where you want to be? Think about your priorities. Have they changed and do you need to alter your life goals accordingly? Sometimes we can doggedly follow a dream even when that dream no longer sparkles for us. This month is also great for planning a long trip.

Friday 21 January

You can maintain your objectivity today in the face of any emotionally charged situation. People will come to you for advice and counselling for this reason. This month will bring many challenges of a political nature and you should try to keep yourself up-to-date with local or regional issues. Ring your mum to get the gossip about the rest of the family.

Saturday 22 January

With the air full of higher vibrations, by all means, call up a few friends and get together for a laugh and a wine, but try to maintain your conversational footing to keep your reputation intact. There will be an event in the home that irritates you but it may be a retaliation due to past mistakes. In that case you should swallow your anger and try to make amends through kindness.

Sunday 23 January

Time to take a good hard look at your relationships and partnerships, and don't be content to accept everything without question. You have your own ideas and plans, and if you put up with delays then you might miss some valuable opportunities. If you are frustrated with the lack of imagination in others, maybe you're are not playing the role of the social stimulant to the degree you have in the past.

Monday 24 January

Life is taking on the feel of a freeway at peak hour, and finding a safe place to pull over may elude you. You have to find a means to express your feelings when everyone is too busy to think of anyone else. Today's planetary aspects focus on communication, so perhaps talking over your ideas or writing to someone whose insight you value will do the trick. Even doodling can give you a place to put your thoughts.

Tuesday 25 January

Progress towards your lunar goal should be reaching its zenith today with the appearance of a full Moon. Take advantage of its abundant energies to push forward. While there is a general understanding that you are busy and probably already do what you can, some things won't suddenly fix themselves in the meantime. Ignore important tasks at your peril. Excuses won't stand up.

Wednesday 26 January
Your social life is really kicking along and you are in two minds about whether the trend is good for you. You have squandered much time making spontaneous house calls and conversations over coffee, and you've taken it away from your hobbies or your housework. You need to reassess your priorities and if push comes to shove, you need to learn to say no.

Thursday 27 January
You are talking about your career and your ambitions, but secretly you're aware that love is the greatest reward you can earn. Moral qualities you have developed in your character will put you in a good position to attract the sort of person that could make you very happy. You may find that communication is difficult, so always remember that silence is romantic, too.

Friday 28 January
An interesting day for you lies ahead as Mars aligns with Pluto in your relationships sector. Your energy meets the potential for big change, so whatever happens, it will be of your own divination. It could be as simple as deciding to get to know a friend a little better, or as life-changing as asking your partner to marry you. Whatever it is, make your decision responsibly.

Saturday 29 January
Your vibrant mind will be put to great use in the service of others, but along with dynamic ideas and solutions you have a penchant for the occasional wacky idea. You could try and focus your mental energy on the needs of others,

which will help to keep you grounded in reality. The application of willpower will be difficult at this time, but this is the downside of your laterally leaning mind.

Sunday 30 January

As Mercury joins the Sun in your philosophy sector, you will find your ability to think clearly about your beliefs is increased. Your inclination to overlook the impact of negative forces means that what was a minor fix-up job has turned into a major public relations exercise. Don't expect others to come rushing to your aid, especially when you ignored good advice that ran contrary to your plans.

Monday 31 January

Be very careful about how you treat your friends, remember that they are to be loved, not used. You also may find that those around you are focussed on the material world to the exception of everything else. Can you set them straight? It might be best left up to them, especially if you find yourself on the receiving end of some nice gifts.

Tuesday 1 February

Be very careful what you choose to believe in, or even whom you choose to trust to know the facts. That is, don't give the charlatan the keys to the kingdom, especially when the king is sleeping in the counting house. Money, sensuality and health can be a focus at this time, and travel may help to decide an outcome. Gurus and ideologies of one kind or another cannot provide answers to your questions.

Wednesday 2 February

As the Moon wanes to darkness in the sky, you should be wrapping up the final details on your lunar goal. Remember to tie up any of the loose ends that could bring you undone. While it might be OK to go along with the crowd if you've nothing better to do, trying to gauge the ultimate intentions of such people may reveal more than you expected.

Thursday 3 February

As Venus moves into your learning sector, you will find beauty in understanding a little more about the world around you. Mankind may never organise itself into some sort of Utopian society, but each successive political movement achieves something and so you should focus on what you can achieve rather than being deluded by the big picture.

Friday 4 February

A new relationship will leave you intimidated. If you find infatuation a little scary, you might want to back out now before you actually fall in love – or maybe it's too late. Meeting someone new can be unsettling, especially when you are utterly entranced by his or her looks or grace. Other areas of your life will lack your attention, although there is no danger in taking a little holiday from the same old same old.

Saturday 5 February

A new romantic interest that you meet in an art gallery or a bank could very well generate the feeling of love at first sight. Creativity and ingenuity are highlighted today, especially in your career, but don't let yourself become self-indulgent with the taste of success. A strong sense of colour will be of good use in the arts. You may have issues with seeking perfection in your relationships – cosmetic surgery can only achieve so much.

Sunday 6 February

Stability will enter your life and will bring a sense of permanence into your world. Once you have your home base established, go where there is no path and leave a trail. If you are resolved to find a way for yourself you will always find opportunities, and if you don't find them, you will make them. This is an important way to refresh your self-image as a better version than the one that preceded it

Monday 7 February

There is a sense of dread about the passing of your days. Try to unlearn your sense of time, because time is conceptual and awareness of it does not need to be maintained. There is a large amount of work on your plate – if you feel like screaming, you're not alone. Experience has taught you to keep your head down and immerse yourself in the job at hand, and there are opportunities to work in a team.

Tuesday 8 February

Until mid-March you receive a boost of energy that you can put to good use in your financial situation. The appearance of a new Moon means an opportunity to embark on a new adventure. Think carefully about what you want to achieve in the long-term. Decide where you should put your energies this lunar month and sketch out a plan of attack.

Wednesday 9 February

Today is a day for pleasing yourself, getting involved in whatever takes you fancy. Others will enjoy tagging along for the ride, so it might a real hoot. The only thing to watch out for is someone who is intent on bringing you down, because they would rather see others miserable than lift themselves out of the doldrums. Being inclusive can put such people off their game for long enough to matter.

Thursday 10 February

You have a very dynamic personality that attracts those around you, even if you doubt it at first. Try bringing people together to do something of your choice for a change, as you may regret missing the chance. You have been quite busy lately and this has had a negative effect on your family life. Today is a good chance to strengthen some of those connections to your children or your partner.

Friday 11 February

You need as many friends at the moment, preferably with similar motives, to help you achieve some important goals. Money might be a factor in your overall success, but keep your lateral mind open if you can. While you exhibit an easy-going, go-with-the-flow attitude, you'll always wear your heart on your sleeve. You crave a lover who can protect you and make you feel safe.

Saturday 12 February

Your social life could be very, very hectic, so be warned. Enjoy your day by making the most of opportunities. The tendency for people to act or react too quickly or impulsively, and the possibility of being overgenerous with time and money, is in the stars. There may be deeper reasons why this issue has surfaced again, which would merit your time and attention. See the event as an opportunity to clear up any old debts, both in terms of money and emotional knots that may yet need untying.

Sunday 13 February

There is an opposition between your head and your heart, and in the end you will need to concentrate on the good in your life and revel in the moments of peace. It is during our darkest moments that we must focus to see the path ahead. Strength is born in the deep silence of long-suffering hearts rather than in the happy whoops of joy. So long pain to wash over you and strip your leaves like the new winter.

Monday 14 February

As the Sun and Mercury form a conjunction in your education sector today, you can expect to be a little muddle-minded, especially when it comes to lending and borrowing money. It's like trying to read a book in the very bright sunshine. Your thoughts are firing on all cylinders with too much illumination. Try to waylay any major assignments or talks until tomorrow.

Tuesday 15 February

Venus and Neptune align in your social conscience area of your life today; meaning your dreams for an improved world can be better actualised. We are genetically programmed to associate with others and from this comes the pack mentality. A mistake is forgivable, but you should know better than to repeat one. You are having trouble motivating yourself to complete a major project and there is an impulse to abandon it altogether.

Wednesday 16 February

Fuelled by a little daydreaming, your energy and passion for life will be at an all-time high over the next few days. Your enthusiasm may have you tripping over your tongue, especially with friends. You have an urge to spend up on beautiful things and big ideas. You will need to decide if it is better to splurge a little, or whether you should try to be conservative with your money.

Thursday 17 February

Mercury has moved into your careers sector for the next couple of weeks, meaning you will thinking a lot about your ambitions and how you can increase your status at work. You are annoyed that someone has not succeeded in fulfilling your expectations of their abilities. Whether it is a child or a work colleague involved, you need to change your attitude in the same way.

Friday 18 February

Even if yours is a simple desk job, you can use your bridge to the dream world to enhance your everyday tasks. Daydreams are never humdrum but your wistful wonderings are epic in their scope. You must have confidence in your imaginings to bring them into your daily life. If you are in the arts or the sciences, you could have some real 'eureka!' moments.

Saturday 19 February

Your career is highlighted for you this month. The Sun shines brightly onto your personal ambitions, and it is a good time to make moves on that promotion or get yourself noticed in the classroom. Don't be shy. It is your time to shine. Put yourself forward for something that would ordinarily make you nervous, such as public speaking, and reap the rewards.

Sunday 20 February

As Mercury, the planet of communication, comes into alignment with Uranus, the planet of originality, in your career sector today, you will find you are wired for interesting solutions to long-standing problems, especially when it comes to making your own ambitions a reality. There is the need to keep things to yourself due to the selfish motives of those who will get ahead at any cost.

Monday 21 February

You sometimes feel separated from your daily environment. Today you must work towards a balance between this outer world and your inner feelings. In this way you will begin to feel much more in harmony with yourself. Your ego has been hidden recently and you are feeling very secretive, especially with your family. This is not apparent to the outside world, however, and your friends and family are enjoying your company.

Tuesday 22 February

Today is the beginning of a highly sociable couple of days for you. While your sparkling social repartee is wooing them, your shy aspect may be masked in excessive alcohol consumption or other unhealthy practices. Parties will be a feature and you will enjoy flirting and chatting with friends. Directing your energy into conversation, it may be the best time to talk over some of those ideas you have been considering.

Wednesday 23 February

There is a problem that you have been considering for some time. It is time that you shared this with a friend. Also, you may meet someone in a romantic sense. They will have an impact on you for some time. The party atmosphere continues and this meeting is one product of your socialising. Remember that a friend is someone who knows us but decides to keep on loving us anyway.

Thursday 24 February

As a full Moon burns bright in the sky it is time to consider whether your lunar goal is making the progress it should be. It is a good day for getting into the nit-picky detail and ironing out the folds. After the fun and frivolity, you have lots of energy for taking on work for others and will do some good turns for close friends and family.

Friday 25 February

The party is ending. A barrier will be put up in your work life and it will need to be broken down in an unpredictable fashion. This shift is confined to your work, not your career as such, so the ripples are contained. Try to remember that friends may come and go, but enemies accumulate. This is pertinent advice for someone entering the phase you are tonight.

Saturday 26 February

Work will continue to impinge on your state of mind and the meaning of yesterday's occurrences will only become apparent today. Your ability to express yourself is going to be an important tool as you negotiate some of these hurdles. You should have no trouble putting your case forward, but there will always be something that you are hiding, even from yourself. Hold firm and you will come through.

Sunday 27 February

As Venus moves into Pisces, you will find yourself really enjoying getting ahead at work and making a good impression on the boss. Use this attractive time to your advantage. Don't get carried away with anger over being wronged because, with focused effort, there is more to be gained than getting a few grievances off your chest. Choose your battles wisely.

Monday 28 February

Saturn is having a rough time, so you will find disciplining yourself, especially when it comes to your material desires, really tough today. Shopping will become almost irresistible, but should not be indulged in if you can help it. You do not have the willpower right now to keep to your budget. You might also find yourself being greedy at the expense of someone who needs it more.

Tuesday 1 March

It is time to start redressing the balance between work and home. This period continues to be about work, but you are shifting your focus towards your relationships. This is good timing as an important relationship will go through a change of some sort today. Your devil-may-care attitude belies the fixed nature of someone who is most comfortable when there is calm; don't panic just yet.

Wednesday 2 March

Philosophically, you are experiencing a sharp learning curve. You are beginning to see things that have been hidden from you for some time. The upheaval of the last few days in the workplace begins to settle and you are entering into a new phase in your relationships, both in business and pleasure. You will need to keep a firm grip on the rudder to steer this boat.

Thursday 3 March

The last quarter of the Moon brings new urgency to the task at hand. On this emotionally charged day, this is especially great as the tense lunar aspects mean you are finding everything a little more difficult than you would normally.

Keep a balanced outlook on life that understands the equally important roles of aggressive and passive energy. In your own life you are in a constant battle to accept what happens to you.

Friday 4 March
There are two major influences at work in the heavens today. One is the move of Mercury into your social sector, meaning you will be thinking in more abstract ways. The other is Venus and Uranus coming together in your career sector. This will give you greater capacity to put yourself across as the attractive and viable alternative. Combine these two energies to put yourself forward for that promotion you deserve.

Saturday 5 March
If you are single, you should try to take advantage of your attractive aura and do a little constructive flirting. Remember, there is a difference between constructive and destructive flirting. If you are careful about who you flirt with and manage to stay light-hearted about things, you will be fine. Your benevolent exterior is attracting the most marvellous conversation. If you are in a relationship, consider an impromptu dinner date a game of scrabble.

Sunday 6 March
You may confuse your partner today by running hot and cold as your desire to please switches place with your need to appear independent and like a person of the world. There is a danger that you could end up fighting over a trivial matter. You should try to focus your emotional energy into your partnership at this time and lavish your loved one with attention.

Monday 7 March
The idea to take an overseas trip may come upon you from nowhere today. There will be an inclination to find yourself through exploration of a wider nature and a trip to the

shops just won't cut it. This may be a fleeting feeling, but it is part of a wider exploration of your personality. Take it as it comes rather than making any fixed and final plans at this stage.

Tuesday 8 March

It is a good day to take a short trip and get rid of some restless energy that may find you in trouble. You may even create that trouble yourself today with a tactless comment or by engaging in an argument with a little too much force. Take a step back if you feel the temperature rising and make sure you don't say anything you will regret.

Wednesday 9 March

You are in touch with your spiritual side and prophetic dreams are a possibility. Avoid any activity that forces you to be grounded in materialism rather than the ether. If your dreams carry a hefty price tag, you might not be in the right frame of mind. Try to protect yourself from psychic vampirism, as you are not strong enough in your mind today to protect against deceitful hangers-on.

Thursday 10 March

The dawn of a new Moon brings with it the opportunity to start again. What will be your lunar goal this month? It's well worth being patient with your subconscious in these situations because your conscious mind can easily suppress your true feelings with the weight of logic. Try to be firm with friends who want your time for themselves, unless of course that is the way you relax.

Friday 11 March

Friends are a good sounding board for some of your more harebrained thoughts. If you are feeling a little down today, it may be a good idea to make an impromptu visit. Take a little gift with you, maybe a bottle of wine, and this could be the perfect opportunity to vent some of those

thoughts. This is the beginning of a period of soul searching that will have many benefits.

Saturday 12 March

For the next week or so, you will be beset by self-doubt.
There may even be some recriminations to deal with – not
very pleasant, but the sort of accountability for a bad decision that we all have to deal with at one point or another.
Confrontational behaviour will take over you at times – try
to direct this impulsive little sprite into a more constructive
outlet.

Sunday 13 March

You will be spoiling for a fight today, and if you aren't
careful you might get more than you bargained for. On the
positive side, your mental self is now in the same ballpark
as your inner ideals, so you may be able to communicate
your thoughts with more clarity. Try not to let yourself
become frustrated if you are not immediately understood;
remain patient if you can.

Monday 14 March

Emotionally, you are craving some tangible toy that will
represent your success. This is not necessarily a bad thing,
as long as you remember that the toy is not your goal. The
toy is only a manifestation of your emotional means. Buy
something nice, but not too expensive. An even better idea
would be to make something for yourself, a picture frame,
a waste paper bin; perhaps you could decorate the fridge?

Tuesday 15 March

You have massive amounts of emotional energy to funnel
into constructive or destructive outcomes today. Your focus
will be the key to a good use of this energy. Attention is
fixed firmly either on your friends, in which case the issue
will be of an emotional nature, or on family, and you may
be a bit obstinate in trying to change a situation. Try to
compromise.

Wednesday 16 March

Ask yourself questions about what hinders you and what helps you. It is important to search for honest answers. Take the phone off the hook and put on some music. Have a good think about all the stuff the busyness of everyday life keeps from you. Perhaps make a list and keep it in a private place. Come back to that list in a week or two.

Thursday 17 March

Your lunar goal should be well under way. Saturn has stalled in your house of material goodies and money, which is probably a good thing since it has been a long time going backward. You may have felt like you were going nowhere in this area, and this feeling is not likely to let up for at least another week. Don't let the frustration get to you, though. Relief is imminent.

Friday 18 March

Clear thought and analysis are the keys to solving the emotional problems that have been troubling you. Keep your eyes open and the opportunity to do this may be handed to you on a platter. It has been a difficult couple of days. Your melancholy mood will continue, but your desire to sink the boot in at any opportunity is leaving – your friends and family sigh with relief!

Saturday 19 March

There is a saying: having a breakdown to have a break-through. Your mind and emotions still feel as though they are dealing with yesterday's news. This may be blinding you to ways you can make simple changes for numerous benefits. If this weight has been slowly building recently, it may be the perfect time to have a little cry. Again, take the phone off the hook and put on some music.

Sunday 20 March

Mars is moving into your education sector over the next few days, which means added energy to this area of your life. This could be hindered by Mercury going retrograde, which means communications go astray and things get lost in translation. There is chatter all around you right now, but you may not be getting into the groove conversation-wise.

Monday 21 March
The Sun has moved into your social conscience, which means your are shining in your outer social sphere this month. Your ability to communicate to a wide audience is heightened at this time. Put this energy into the science or welfare sectors for its greatest effect. Hitting upon unusual solutions to old problems and lateral thinking in general is now accessible to you.

Tuesday 22 March
Today is not the day for argumentative point scoring; there is a lesson to be learned. Tension with your partner may be inevitable; only, the result is under your control. Your unconscious mind is undermining your conscious will and there is a dichotomy there for all except you to see. Be careful you don't turn up the emotional volume; listen and think about what it is people are trying to point you to.

Wednesday 23 March
If you don't normally buy the newspaper, do so today. You will be in the mood for sparkling conversation and the newspaper may offer the fuel that you require. Remember, opinions are like bellybuttons, everybody has one. Don't be too opinionated in your conversation and listen to what others have to say as well. There are sure to be interesting insights if you have your ears open.

Thursday 24 March
Today there will be an unusual purchase to be made. The things that you have dismissed from your wish list may turn out to be a real possibility. However, you should refrain from any short-term business dealing that relies on

your judgment. This includes trading shares or on the spot deals that you haven't time to check thoroughly. You are more than likely to do yourself out of some cash.

Friday 25 March

Venus is on the march through your social sector, so don't be surprised if you are attracted to more unusual types right now. The full Moon has bought a sense of urgency to the completion of your lunar goal. Don't dilly dally, especially as Saturn is coming out of hiding in your money sector tomorrow, freeing up a little cash and letting you achieve what you need to.

Saturday 26 March

Giving away someone else's money is not a good idea at the best of times, but your judgment about who is needy and who is scamming is right off. You could find yourself giving away someone else's money with all the good intentions in the world – don't. It's a good day for your children to ask for more pocket money (but don't tell them that!)

Sunday 27 March

Diplomacy and a poetic ear will woo those people who have been against you in the past. This will please you no end. While all of the cards appear to be out on the table, someone may be dealing from the bottom of the deck. Use your words as your defence and you should have no trouble negotiating the problems of the day.

Monday 28 March

You are having a bit of a charmed shopping week in general and today is no exception. You are particularly attractive and hard to resist when it comes to money, particularly asking for it. This is the time to ask for that raise if it is overdue. In fact, your charismatic bargaining could save you money. If you were putting off a big purchase, now is the day to bite the bullet.

Tuesday 29 March

There are some powerful energies colliding over the next three days in your social sector, and the result is quite unpredictable. Clarity could be yours when it comes to humanitarian causes, or confusion could reign supreme. Try to keep a level head. Always give more help to those who help themselves and reward those who go beyond the call of duty and take on responsibility.

Wednesday 30 March

You are beginning to suspect that one of your bargain purchases on your shopping spree was not such a bargain after all. The superficiality and the materialism of the last few days have reversed and you should start communicating on a more straightforward level. You will find emotional satisfaction from your workmates, but it is not enough to override the fact that work is grating against you.

Thursday 31 March

Intuition in most mere mortals is the culmination of all senses making subtle judgments. It is rarely a supernatural event. With this in mind, psychic impressions and errant thoughts should be kept in check today. A rational mind and process of elimination is not always the way to treat a gut feeling, but today you should be extra careful about your intuition. Question your first impressions.

Friday 1 April

As the Sun and Mercury come together in your social sector, expect to speak your mind, especially when it comes to social issues. While things are going well with your work, you are wondering whether it's time to think about your next major adventure. If things are OK financially, it is time to consider an adventure of a different kind.

Saturday 2 April

As Pluto goes retrograde in your relationships sector, you could find that the change you were looking for in this area goes on hold. Your spiritual life has perhaps been neglected and it's the perfect time to resume the journey of your soul by seeking cultural and religious interests. Feeling this good about your ideas and your potential to shape your social environment for the better can only be a good thing.

Sunday 3 April

Life refuses to be embalmed and so should you. If you are trying to watch TV and the phone keeps ringing, you should get the message. You are feeling pretty good about your physical presence and will have no trouble using your confidence to shift a few mountains out of your way. Why you are not taking the utmost of this advantage is not clear.

Monday 4 April

You are seeking mental stimulation and you might find yourself restlessly putting down books and picking them up again. You are trying to quench your thirst for something new to think about. You comprehend ways to open your mind by combining your drive and energy with your ability to think, although you're putting a lot of this energy into your domestic situation. Find your focus.

Tuesday 5 April

As Jupiter duels with the Sun and Mercury in your romance sector, you could find that the lucky break you were looking for proves to be even more elusive. You're having a bit of trouble holding onto your hard-earned pennies, although you don't feel you're spending excessive amounts on recreation. It is time that your tongue was unleashed to let fly a few well-placed arrows.

Wednesday 6 April

Regardless of how personal your work relationships seem to get, there is always a line that is crossed at your own risk. You may need to develop a personal list of conversation and email topics that are off limits. Some people do not have the confidence to confront others, so the issue could simmer or go to a higher level – something no one wants to happen.

Thursday 7 April

Connecting with people on a deeper level than usual is important to you. You should intuitively know whether or not it's 'meant to be' when you meet someone new. Ambivalence is often misused as a synonym for apathetic. It really means that you swing between love and hate, yes and no, happiness and sadness about the issue in question. People can have conflicting impulses – remember that today.

Friday 8 April

Decide today where you want to devote your energies over the next lunar month. The new Moon brings a fresh beginning. When things are going your way, they really go your way. You are in fine form today and no fortunate circumstance is too fortunate. Be open to charity, even if it's just an offering of time, because it is most satisfying when things are going well.

Saturday 9 April

Your strength and patience will pay off in the long run. One problem at a time and no more and you will get through, but you could feel like the day is longer than it should be. It may be time for you to actively express your feelings. Relax, nothing is as bad as it seems. Keep your composure and deal with each issue as it arises.

Sunday 10 April

At some point there needs to be mutual effort put into reconnecting your major relationship. This may come through socialising. Have you become frustrated at the lack of emotional warmth found in your central relationships? This is not necessarily a bad thing, and you and your friends or partner experience a great deal of growth in your interactions.

Monday 11 April
Perhaps the need to earn more cash quickly encourages you to try for a better-paid job or to achieve that promotion? It could push you into a second job that will take your energy away from where you want it to be. If you make any compromises between what you would like to be and what you have been told is your station, you will lose out.

Tuesday 12 April
If possible, try to give yourself plenty of space to deal with a dramatic event in your social life. It may mean that you cannot devote as much time to socialising as you would like, which will be frustrating. The majority of today's pleasure will come via entertaining yourself with your favourite hobbies, releasing the emotional pressures of the day.

Wednesday 13 April
Mars and Neptune complete a pas de deux in your education sector today, meaning you will be able to work towards your dreams to further your studies. Some conflict may arise between you and anyone who projects negative circumstances onto their life through pessimism. Any arrogance will work against you.

Thursday 14 April
If you feel the need to catch up on a little intellectual conversation, this is your chance. You will have plenty of opportunities to talk to all the right people, not only if you are out socialising with friends, but also in a professional environment. Perhaps there are some political issues that you thought you understood quite well, but now you need to clear up the details.

Friday 15 April

Lifestyle and location changes mean it is difficult to make the idea of 'friends forever' a reality. But we can develop intimate relationships with one or a few people, and these equate to the friendship of many in terms of quality. As you get older you find that friends can drop off, never to be seen again.

Saturday 16 April

As Venus moves into your subconscious, beauty becomes hidden from you over the next few weeks. Romance could appear in the guise of an unsolved mystery. A few clues might lead you to love. Relax and you will find joy in the most surprising places. People working in large institutions, such as hospitals, will find this energy most beneficial.

Sunday 17 April

Part of the rift between science and spirituality is the idea that the two describe the same thing – and that one is right and the other is wrong. The weight of your spiritual belief is enough to keep your eyes focused on a particular way of living. You risk neglecting the need to work through problems in a rational way, rather than looking to the spirit world for divine intervention and wisdom.

Monday 18 April

You need to be careful not to push things along too quickly today, particularly in relationships. Forcing verbalised feelings or tacky material offerings are out. You want to get things moving, but you are afraid that your feelings are not reciprocated. Things will only be spoilt by rushing them. If you are patient, the result you wish for will come to you.

Tuesday 19 April

Your common sense could have you whistling all the way to the bank. As your loftier aspirations seem to gather steam, you should temper this by becoming less ethereal and more real. When left on your own to exercise you may become lazy and reluctant. To engage in exercise seems a lonely business you quickly become bored with, so engaging in a team sport is a good idea.

Wednesday 20 April

As the Sun moves into Taurus, you will find yourself in a more reflective and contemplative mood. In the lead up to your birthday next month, this is a good time to consider what the year before has held for you and what you would like to achieve in the following year. Don't press yourself into attending many engagements if you don't feel like it. Take things quietly if that's what feels right.

Thursday 21 April

The way that you and your partner coordinate work and play, and the private and the public spheres, will define the people you are becoming. In unexpected ways, you may be subject to a dramatic event that puts you under emotional stress. You have picked up excellent coping skills over the last few years, but the real measure of your resilience is the way you keep focused on critical aspects of your life.

Friday 22 April

Your magnanimous attitude will put you in the good books with children because they don't deal well with concealing emotions. In fact, everybody will see you coming a mile away. So, don't organise important meetings that require delicate negotiations, as your communication skills are currently more like a bull in a china shop. Conversely, others are caught up in your buoyant spirit and interesting ideas.

Saturday 23 April

The lines of communication are once again open and you are able to say what you really mean and have it heard with open ears and forgiving hearts. Seize the opportunity. You have been misconstrued and taken out of context, and your reputation may have been sullied. However, your character remains intact and it is time to put measures in place to defend yourself.

Sunday 24 April

The pregnant Moon wends its way across the sky tonight, signalling the zenith of your lunar energy. Don't be afraid to take on way more than you can reasonably chew because this will maximise the benefits to be gained over the next few days. That said, saying yes to absolutely everything will not be your smartest move. Try minimum input for maximum output.

Monday 25 April

Your best bet is to just let go, drift in and out of the waves of the cosmic sea for a bit, and see if you can find peace instead. You will be happiest with your children. Communication is the other main area of focus, and it seems you will be very busy. You should be wary of all sorts of crazy conspiracy theories coming your way today.

Tuesday 26 April

If you look back on recent events you will find that you invite criticism by appearing to lack emotional maturity. There are so many people in your face when it comes to understanding your current relationships that you wonder whether they know your partner better than you do. Setting the boundaries for subjects that are off-limits is not impossible but can take a while.

Wednesday 27 April

Most work relationships are not like friendships because people are forced into proximity against their own wishes. But where there is trust and respect, there is also potential to develop something more than a purely utilitarian relationship. Things that you have learnt in the home will strike you as being universal in nature and with a little ingenuity they will apply to your work situation.

Thursday 28 April

Perhaps it is a good day to take your kids to the beach or somewhere fun, where you can enjoy their company. If you don't have children, you could always give a grateful mum a break and spend some time with your nieces, nephews, grandkids or godchildren. You are the Pied Piper for once and you should have no trouble gaining the attention of youthful minds.

Friday 29 April

Although you are right to have the conviction of your opinions, you might choose appropriate social moments to air them. You are feeling strongly about some political issue and occasionally you are revealing this to the people you work with. If the issue is very contentious, you may run the risk of forcing people to take sides, which will potentially create division and stimulate gossip.

Saturday 30 April

You are too swayed by your emotions right now. Coupled with your inability to read the mood of the moment in your house, you could end up involved in a big barney that no one will win. Try not to get involved in any domestic disputes today as you will lose, and quite possibly show yourself to be the fool, or worse yet, a gossip.

Sunday 1 May

As Mars moves into your career sector, you will find your energy is best directed by focussing on your more ambitious plans. Your boss has been given his marching orders and you will have reserves of energy over the coming weeks to act upon your ambitions. Try not to step on any toes while you get there. Remember that the people that you climb over on the way up, are the same people who will catch you on your way down.

Monday 2 May

You may have trouble getting through to someone close to you today. Your first impulse is to feel resentment because you know what could be achieved with cooperation. Instead, you will need patience and a little distance from the situation to find a creative and effective solution. With those close to you, communication will come in time.

Tuesday 3 May

If you have been involved in arguments lately, there will be a chance to clear the air today. There are ways and means to get what you want from someone but it won't help your cause to be perceived as manipulative. While negotiations may ensue, it is better that you leave your poker face where it is. In a clash of minds, the only outcome you can accept is a trade-off.

Wednesday 4 May

Have you forgotten about an old debt? There is some sort of fiscal responsibility that will catch up with you today. Take a moment to get this sorted out before you do anything else and you might find a series of unexpected, positive repercussions. One of these may be renewed contact with a long forgotten acquaintance. The relationship could pick up right where it left off.

Thursday 5 May

Your communication levels are at their height and you will be able to say whatever it is that needs to be said, with absolute conviction and clarity. Employ the abilities of those around you and you may achieve a great deal. Maintain fairness and freedom as your watchwords and you will have an opportunity to go in for the underdog, especially if they are children.

Friday 6 May

Maintain a picture of where you are headed to ensure that you don't get worn down. You have already been through upheavals regarding your home, and yet you still may not be satisfied with where the tide has washed you. You might want to try and sort matters out once and for all. Push to get yourself into exactly the situation that you have wanted to be in for so long.

Saturday 7 May

You have to balance the need to trust the universe and dive in the deep end with the need to consider that there really could be a shark in the swimming pool. A very big decision is required soon, which will affect the way people perceive you. Remember, there are no right and wrong decisions and chances are high you'll make a positive choice.

Sunday 8 May

A new Moon offers a chance to try again. Work out your lunar goal for this month and resolve to make a difference. You'll have some trouble cooperating in a group setting because your impulse will be to set your own pace. You are out of touch with your feelings as the weight of work drags you down.

Monday 9 May

Try to be a little dignified, man! Do what you need to do and then go back to relative anonymity. You may have to face the fact that no one will be taking this task off your hands in a hurry. You don't like to have the wants and needs of others under your care, but in this situation there is not much you can do about it.

Tuesday 10 May

As the planetary ball plays on, a quick glance at your dance card has your heart skipping a beat. The lovely Venus has waltzed into your sign and you can expect your life to be filled with all her gorgeous qualities. Over the coming weeks, your presence will be more attractive, and your words and gestures more convincing in their aesthetic quality. The finer things in life become more important and you will be more focussed on material things.

Wednesday 11 May

It is sometimes difficult to remember that you know nothing for sure, except the fact that you know nothing for sure. Sometimes, even that is up for grabs. You will need to gather your resources today so that you don't say no just to hear the sound of your own voice. To be effective you must understand that efforts and bravery are not enough without purpose and direction.

Thursday 12 May

Things may be working with you rather than against you at the moment, so don't hold back. New and unusual ways of appreciating and loving may be possible now. You might even discover something unexpected, or you might adopt a different and unconventional value system for a time. This is an excellent period to make decisions and to take care of mental work.

Friday 13 May

Your brain moves into a lower gear today as Mercury parks in the sector of your subconscious. You are likely to find your communication skills a little sluggish over the next month, and you will have to work hard to make yourself understood. You may even unwittingly reveal a sworn secret or offend someone with a slip of the tongue. Cryptic puzzles and detective games are good fun and it's time to do some investigative work.

Saturday 14 May

Set your goals overly high so you extend yourself by trying to achieve them. Don't be too disappointed if you don't reach your exact goals. Take a moment to look around and assess just what you have achieved. Try not to create a false self-image. Look for clues in the way your loved ones react to your behaviour and then adjust your aim accordingly.

Sunday 15 May

Working towards your deepest dreams and desires is given a helping hand today as Mars and Neptune join forces in your career sector today. This is especially true if your desires revolve around your ambitions, or in the areas of business or helping the elderly. Although you crave a physical break, not to mention a mental one, you will be better served by seeing the job at hand finished in good time.

Monday 16 May

You will need to improvise today because your best-laid plans will be thrown to the wind by everyone around you. Keep all the information close at hand and you will be able to negotiate every problem and task that is set for you. You will be the well that everybody approaches with their questions. Find that text book of yours and throw it out the window today.

Tuesday 17 May

Sigh with relief, by all means, but take the opportunity to complete the task properly in the relaxed environment you have been given. You won't get a second chance to redeem yourself. Someone from your past issues a challenge you can't gracefully refuse. The limitations of a new technological innovation will give you the excuse you need when you are questioned about something you should have done months ago.

Wednesday 18 May

Remember that you could easily be on the receiving end of your own solution. Have you laid an intricate plan with the goal of entrapment or making someone else look foolish – a colleague perhaps? There is a good chance that the only mouse to be caught in your trap today will be yourself. Openness and honesty are the best policies for you.

Thursday 19 May

You have a choice to subscribe to a type of intellectual elitism, or maintain relative obscurity by donating your time and money to causes that seek to make a difference. Commitment to antiquated notions of an idealised past never broke a chain or freed a human soul and never will. At the same time, modern ideals can also fail to make a mark on the world.

Friday 20 May

You are nagged by the sense that you are missing out on time with your friends through commitment to your career. Such concerns fall away when you are able to provide for your partner or children and experience the satisfaction of parenthood. You are excelling at your job at the moment and this will put you in line for a pay increase or a promotion. Is this the reward you deserve?

Saturday 21 May

Happy birthday Gemini! The Sun has entered your sign, which means you have a whole month to shine. Your ego is benefiting from the warm rays of the largest celestial body in our galaxy, and there will be a bigger, brighter, more ebullient you. This self-confidence seeps into all areas of your life, so expect to make a prominent mark on business, relationships, friends and family.

Sunday 22 May

This is your time to concentrate on more meditative and speculative endeavours. A little free time for the mind is long overdue, and while you seem busy you will find quiet moments at the most surprising times. Don't be fooled into thinking that daydreaming is a waste of time, but be sure to productively employ the fruits of your whimsy. You will be pleasantly surprised.

Monday 23 May

A golden orb fills the sky, with energy radiating like the vibrations from a well-struck cymbal. Assess where you are on your lunar path and adjust the course if the conditions are not right. You and your partner may need to be reminded that when agreeing to a relationship, you commit to the work required to smooth the way.

Tuesday 24 May
As soon as you can learn to relax, there is nothing stopping a new relationship from progressing. So, try to switch your brain off and enjoy the good feelings. You have devoted yourself to a person, or are at least to trying to secure the attention of someone and it is working. If you are finding it hard to leave your expectations at the door, this will prove an impediment.

Wednesday 25 May
You can only be all things to all people if you are nothing to yourself, and that is what you are finding yourself left with right now. In trying to please everybody you are really trying to please yourself. Take a moment today to do a checklist of all your parts – arms, head, body and legs. All accounted for? Now take them all out for a boogie.

Thursday 26 May
Are you finding that many of your friends cannot empathise well with your situation? Take a little time to renew your relationships with your siblings; it has been too long since you relived old times. Also, you are in line for a financial gain, providing you are open to the idea of giving in order to get. It may be a matter of meeting someone's financial needs without the promise of any return, but be careful.

Friday 27 May
Faith goes up the stairs that love builds and looks out windows that hope has opened and finds that you just don't know enough yet to make sense of it all. You will become a scholar yet. No matter where we go, we take a little of each other everywhere and refer back to each other's take on things in times of need.

Saturday 28 May

Make sure you stay well within the spending limit of your charge cards or you could find yourself in trouble. Expect high performance from your helpers, clients and business partners, and you will motivate others to greater heights. You are going to have to let people know what you need from them if they can be any help to you.

Sunday 29 May

As Mercury moves into your sign, you will find you are quite the chatterbox over the coming weeks. Meetings with close friends and encounters with your neighbours will yield interesting results. Expect this month's phone bill to be a bit more expensive than usual and your email box will be running hot. Planning to make a short trip over the coming weeks could prove to be the refreshing change you've been looking for.

Monday 30 May

Sometimes we cannot walk through the mud without getting a certain amount of it stuck to our shoes. There may be some in-fighting today. It will involve gossip and personalities. Your best intentions will be to steer clear of the whole mess. However, you are going to get a little dirty anyway. Do the best that you can and have a long hot shower at the end of the day.

Tuesday 31 May

You decide to take a calculated risk and, whether it's with a client, your boss or an associate, the gamble pays off just as you hoped it would. Whether you see attention as flattery, quality control or dirty espionage, you are just going to have to learn to get on with the job. It's a good time for casual or serious talks with your partner.

Wednesday 1 June

You had to regroup recently as you found that people don't always respond well to direct coercion. Something as simple as letting others have their say can help to make them compliant. You have been learning about the need to submit to other people's ideas and listen to people you don't really respect; with greater understanding of these people will come a measure of respect.

Thursday 2 June

The ego is picking up a little today and that can be a dangerous thing. You might even find yourself talking like a motivation speaker from late night television. If try to be aloof with the people around, no one will gain anything, least of all yourself. When you finally come down from your pedestal you will learn more than you thought you already knew.

Friday 3 June

Don't try to hold onto something so hard or try to push past perceived boundaries without really thinking what it is you are trying to achieve. Drawing negative attention to yourself will have consequences. Your generosity and attractiveness are shining through in your wisdom and knowledgeable air. A great day for romance, but you must be at pains not to do anything silly or impulsive today in this area.

Saturday 4 June

Venus has dropped in for a coffee on her way to the shops and has invited you along. This gracious presence in your money sector will mean an emphasis on materialism over the coming weeks, and you will find shopping and prettying up your environment a main focus. Keep an eye on your purse strings to make sure this frivolous and fun time doesn't send you over your head financially.

Sunday 5 June

You are a conciliator where romance is concerned. Being in love can involve falling hard and all that effort would be shamefully wasted, but it doesn't mean that everything will suddenly be hunky-dory. Someone who you have a lot of respect for and consider a sort of mentor has gone into bat for you and will surprise you with their complimentary remarks.

Monday 6 June

A crisp new Moon unfolds like a freshly minted dollar bill, and it is another opportunity to begin anew. You can keep developing with an open mind. Your passion for learning new things is in high gear and so is your ability to soak up the knowledge. To prevent poor timing, sit on your haunches until issues become clear.

Tuesday 7 June

Your dreams and goals can help you overcome the depression you feel about your job, as well as help focus your energy on something that is worthwhile and not a quick fix. Although it is hard to look beyond your present situation to see a way to satisfy your soul, a little long-term planning is necessary to maintain your sanity.

Wednesday 8 June

Most people don't realise that eccentricity and genius go hand in hand, so you shouldn't worry yourself too much. Of course, there is no need to follow the style advice you are given; it is a free country. You are respected and valued among your colleagues for your fascinating humanitarian ideas and your creative flair, but the same people tell you to get a haircut and a matching tie.

Thursday 9 June

The benevolent presence of Jupiter has been moving backwards through your romance sector, making what should have been a carefree walk an absolute slog. This backwards motion has been reversed today and you will find life in this area much easier. Luck will be yours in love again.

Friday 10 June

Strategies may come and strategies may go, particularly your own. Do you feel like you have a new master plan each day? Put all of your recent plans onto the table and into perspective. If you can find the right approach, you will be able to achieve anything. Create your own happiness wherever and whenever it appears to be missing. This is a gift that you can give to others as well.

Saturday 11 June

The key to real passion is in connecting with that lover who can make vulnerability an attractive option. You will find useful advice after all the dithering and indecision that you have had to endure recently. You tend to seek agreement in your friendly and harmonious way, a real boon in the give and take of partnership. A progressive nonconformist is a blessing in disguise.

Sunday 12 June

Mars makes a strong move into your social sector, ensuring you have copious amounts of energy for those less fortunate than you. This altruistic energy could be put to use in many sectors, but will be most beneficial in the welfare sector. People with science and technology careers can also use this to their advantage. If your enthusiasm is waning, you will find reserves of strength if you choose by looking at things a little differently.

Monday 13 June

As Mercury shakes its booty into your material sector, you will find yourself thinking and talking about money and all the little joys that a full purse can buy. Make sure you keep your musings in check and don't talk yourself into a buying frenzy. Your speech is warm and comforting, and you will have some lovely ideas for entertaining friends.

Tuesday 14 June

There is a duel in the sky between the Sun and Pluto tonight, which could mean one of two things – all or nothing. For some there will be a great change for the ego; for most, there will be nothing at all. Be proactive about finding the root of the problem and identifying it for what it's worth.

Wednesday 15 June

There will be a tendency to fear change in the next few weeks as you become more and more aware of the passing of time and the pressure to relate to the younger generation saps your energy. You may as well give in and stop trying to maintain your ageing belief system in the face of evidence that debunks it.

Thursday 16 June

Ongoing dramas will become frustrating for you because they are not what you want to deal with at work. You believe that it is your responsibility, and that of the other person, to act professionally regardless of personal differences. Don't be afraid to state this case and set rules of engagement before the situation degenerates. The escalation of a dispute between you and a colleague may only be a conflict of personality.

Friday 17 June

If you feel a drive for social change, for a shift towards something of significance, today is the day to lay some groundwork. If focusing on the goal is too distant and abstract, focus on a simpler, more immediate approach. Set up a recycling bin at work, or perhaps organise a group sponsorship for an underprivileged child. Plant some small, yet practical seeds.

Saturday 18 June

You are in the market for a new piece of equipment. Make sure that you buy the best you can afford, as you know you will only be back at the shop next week if you buy something second-rate. Also, even if you rule the roost, rule with an even hand. Your beloved senses your mood and will adapt to it, which is a blessing that shouldn't be taken for granted.

Sunday 19 June
Previously hidden aspects of a key professional situation will reveal themselves today. This information may prove to be ample ammunition to deal with a tricky and unexpected situation. You may not even have to let on exactly what you know. Merely alluding to the fact that you do know could be enough. If you have important things to discuss with your beloved, the energies are there to help enormously.

Monday 20 June
Where there is interest in your abilities, you will be keen to communicate your knowledge. You will find the lines of communication clear and effective. Life has taught you how to protect yourself both physically and mentally. It has also taught you that physical defence is fraught with danger, whereas a mental approach gets much better results. A young person will gain from your wisdom in this regard.

Tuesday 21 June
For someone like you who holds the values and ideals of the world stage as dear as you do your own family, you are taking the current climate of fear and loathing very badly. This should ease soon. While the politicians claim to be taking democracy to the people of the world, they don't seem to be leaving much of it at home.

Wednesday 22 June
As the low red Moon reaches capacity in the sky, take a moment to work out what needs to be done when it comes to your lunar goal. Your material sector is highlighted this

month and you will be in a spendthrift mood. Try to keep
an eye on those pennies. On the plus side, money will seem
to come to your more freely, and don't be surprised if you
come across a small windfall.

Thursday 23 June
Don't be annoyed if someone you are interested in is reti-
cent to make the first move. Your previous behaviour may
have clearly set a boundary that only you can cross. The
pain you have felt for a long time is slowly starting to abate
and will give you the opportunity to regain levels of
friendship that you kept out of bounds through lack
of trust.

Friday 24 June
Others will question your logic and later doubt your commitment, but in the end you will prove that you have the
capacity for great things, even if you are happy with your
small herb garden. Your mind is made up about the course
of action you think you should take and, lucky for you,
you have the mental stamina and willpower to see it
through.

Saturday 25 June
Lately all your little tricks simply haven't been working.
You need to get back to square one and try to find out
where you began going wrong. Only then will your skills
come back stronger than ever. Over the years you've
developed a great deal of confidence in your ability to
read others and it's time to refine this skill again. The
danger is that you will become complacent.

Sunday 26 June
You will be able to speak with flair about what impedes
you in the area of money. You are in a very patriotic mood
today, and may cause an uncomfortable atmosphere if you
demonstrate your feelings to the people around you. One
of society's unwritten rules is that opinions should be kept

to oneself, unless most of the population shares that opinion.

Monday 27 June

Things will seem bad today, but the heavens have placed luck on your side so it all might be OK anyway. The unusual fascinates you and you are rarely caught off guard by abnormal situations or strange people. The reverse of this is that you can feel a little uncomfortable in conservative settings. Good friends and work colleagues will pull you through these situations today.

Tuesday 28 June

Venus and Mercury skip happily, arm in arm, into your communication sector. You can expect to be thinking and talking about close friends in an appealing way over the coming weeks. It is a good time for finding love and friendship over the Internet or on the phone. You may even find romance a little nearer to home as your close friends seem more attractive over the coming weeks.

Wednesday 29 June

Don't confuse your expectations with premonitions. It can be particularly detrimental to build up ideal outcomes only to be disappointed by reality and the flawed nature of those who participate in it. Like it or not, this includes yourself. Try to keep your mind in the present so that you are prepared for whatever comes your way, and then you can work towards the future.

Thursday 30 June

To a certain degree you are in touch with your ability to remain objective, and people come to you for advice and counselling for this reason. It is a politically charged time when you will take much notice of current events and will form thoughts and opinions on the world around you. This month will bring many challenges where your friends and acquaintances are concerned.

Friday 1 July

You feel that you have something controversial to say. If it is a valid explanation, no blame will be fixed on you. You will need to be on your toes so that your fertile imagination does not endow fresh dimensions to a not-so-complex situation. If your partnership with someone is coming under scrutiny, be wise and conservative while dealing with the problem. You may have to face some criticism from close quarters.

Saturday 2 July

An unlikely situation might come close to persuading you to gamble money you don't have. Put your credit card firmly in your back pocket and get a thrill somewhere else. You will find yourself twice as rich for not taking the gamble. Your attention should be directed towards capitalising on the strong foundations you have already laid. You may find that these foundations have an intellectual basis.

Sunday 3 July

No matter how well intentioned, chances are that you are not going to hit the mark as you hoped today. Don't bite off more than you can chew by putting yourself into a restrictive situation – you may not have the will to climb back out again. You are not in the mood for more fun and games, and you will be more than a little peeved if an unwanted invitation interrupts a work session.

Monday 4 July

Don't spend your day looking into the puddles of the past. These puddles will only offer you a limited view of the world. Remember that there is more satisfaction to be found in working towards the future than languishing in the past. However, if you lose sight of the past, you will repeat the same mistakes – and successes. Bury your head in some hard work that may have been deferred for too long.

Tuesday 5 July

You've been whistling your way down the street for a while now, and finally that karma is coming back to teach you a lesson or two. There's more going on here than meets the eye and you should unravel the thread without too much effort. This will be the best time to turn to a friend who has known you for a long time to talk through old issues.

Wednesday 6 July

The new Moon reminds us that adventure is worthwhile and it is meaningful to seek more out of life through your achievements. Take this opportunity to think about where you are headed and where you want to be. Make your lunar goal a small step towards your larger ambitions. With this type of planning, you will find your path becomes clearer. This will require careful thought.

Thursday 7 July

It is generally a quiet time with lots of contemplation. Soon enough, you will be faced with many challenges regarding your subconscious and recent past. This is the time to recoup your energies and make the most of quiet enjoyments. Looking over the past year and thinking about what you have done well and what you could have done better may prove useful.

Friday 8 July

If you have been wanting a more exciting life, you might just get it today. The old adage, beware of what you wish for because it may come true, is something to think about. A do-or-die attitude may lack common sense and you must learn to rein in some of your impulsive responses; at least try to understand them. The drudgery in your relationship will make you consider straying to greener pastures.

Saturday 9 July

Start a new health regime; your body will affirm your decision by feeling better within days. Eat mindfully and stop before you feel full. Entertain a couple of close friends this evening, nothing fancy, and you will find that each other's company will be enough. Long dinner conversations will engage your sense of interest and bring to the fore social concerns you have not considered for some time.

Sunday 10 July

Don't lose sight of your romantic and lofty goals in the glare of the Sun. With regard to love affairs, all that glistens is not necessarily gold. It is quite possible that you are the fool if you have been entranced by the personal wealth of one of your dates. Have the courage to make positive decisions regarding your relationships and your emotional needs.

Monday 11 July

Interesting challenges will prove rewarding if you can couple your higher thinking and strong willpower for concerted amounts of time. The stamina required to achieve this focus will leave you feeling drained. The rewards to be gained will include an increase in confidence, particularly in the social sphere. Remember that these are skills to be mastered over a long time, and you have the stamina to do it.

Tuesday 12 July

You might think that someone is behaving in a certain way towards you because of something that you said, but really they are probably only going about their business. Today you're feeling a little moody and you might find yourself reaching for the tissues when indulging in a little bit of your favourite soap opera, whether on TV or just a part of your life.

Wednesday 13 July

There is a strong possibility that something of importance, perhaps money, will come into your sphere today. Whether it is yours or someone else's is still up in the air.

You could see this event as a signal for a fresh start. Friends and acquaintances are most likely to be affected by this event, but you may find their counsel hard to take.

Thursday 14 July

It is time for you to set the record straight, particularly in regard to other people's misconceptions. Some might see you as moody, gullible or having weak judgment. Paradoxically, people think you are being too overt in your feelings, especially at work. They don't see that your over-assertive behaviour is used to hide the shyness you feel because you put too much stock in what others think of you.

Friday 15 July

Your 'call a spade a shovel' image is beginning to tarnish a little, even with yourself, so why continue with it? Deep down, you've got sensuality to burn and you need to tap into it by allowing a little of your imagination to come to the surface. Set aside some time today to enjoy yourself without the responsibility of children or old folk to look after. Right now, you need the space.

Saturday 16 July

To gain a valuable perspective, take a moment to reflect on how bad things really look on a global scale. There is every chance that circumstances are not so harsh, rather that you are unusually sensitive at the moment to the usual hardships. This does not mean that you should not always expect better things, from yourself as well as others. Whatever the situation might be, there is a path to a positive end.

Sunday 17 July

As Saturn leaves Cancer and enters Leo today, you'll find that some of the problems and hindrances you experienced in maintaining possessions and making money are no longer an issue. In fact, your skills are now greatly improved in this area. It is not all a bed of roses, though. Saturn is poised to enter your communications sector, putting obstacles and tests in your path.

Monday 18 July

You'll feel invigorated today. If the Sun is shining and you're due at work, you'll be forgiven for contemplating an impromptu day off. The least you can do is make a lunch date with some friends and get out. Talk about love, sport or a sudden need for a new suit. Be sure to buy flowers for someone...anyone!

Tuesday 19 July

You will have an emotional encounter with a wise woman today who will reveal a few insights that will get you back on track. Your career might feel like someone is always pulling when you are pushing and vice versa. This is the area you are putting all your efforts into, but your diligence never seems to pay off like it should.

Wednesday 20 July

A humanitarian goal that you originally had in mind could lead you in unexpected directions. Try not to let a degree of fatalism enter into your sums when drawing conclusions from the information at hand. This will lead to mistakes and future recriminations – nothing is set in stone yet! A problem has arisen because an activity that you considered just a hobby has rapidly taken on more importance.

Thursday 21 July

The fulsome breast of La Luna casts its white glow over the world tonight, gently reminding you to move things a step towards your lunar goal. You know that mediocrity requires aloofness to preserve its dignity. Conversely, to be great, you have to engage people. Don't think you can fool yourself and others by pretending that you don't care if you are nowhere near achieving your aim.

Friday 22 July

Your house and home are about to benefit from the beatific presence of Venus as she enters your family sector. This signals a loving time over the coming weeks where you will crave the presence of the familiar. A great time to get some small renovations done around the house, as your aesthetic sensibilities will be heightened when it comes to your immediate surroundings. A family friend could knock on the door with an offer of romance.

Saturday 23 July

The Sun has entered your communications sector this month, so it will be a good time to re-establish contacts with friends and acquaintances that you have let slip. It is also a good month for enjoying short trips. Plan to do some sightseeing close to home. Think of some of the tourist attractions in your area. How many have you visited? This is a great time to explore your corner of the earth.

Sunday 24 July

Mercury has gone retrograde in your communications sector, which means you might find yourself a little tongue-tied with your close friends. Telephones and computers are likely to play up. This glitch in the system will last for the next three weeks. Communications go awry for all astrological signs at this time, so don't feel singled out. Try your best to comprehend others as well as you can.

Monday 25 July

You will find it hard to stay on track with activities that require hard work; the appeal of socialising may prove too strong. Don't hesitate to turn to your friends for assistance, as they have also been in this very situation. In the work place, try to remain non-combative and don't resort to bad-mouthing colleagues behind their backs if you are rejected. Other avenues will soon reveal themselves to you.

Tuesday 26 July

You feel much more inclined to go for what you want rather than allowing other people's preferences to get in the way. You are perhaps trying to make progress in a situation in that won't allow you to move quickly. The result is that you are tempted to change horses in midstream, which is something that would make your grandfather's hair turn grey.

Wednesday 27 July

What you give to your job is recorded in the collective mind, and the atmosphere is constantly pregnant with opportunities that merely need to be born into existence with a turn of the universal screw. The work you put into your career has not paid off lately and it seems that there are no doors to be seen, let alone any that are opening. Time will tell.

Thursday 28 July

Mars is parting the curtain to your subconscious for the next few weeks, which means that your energy reserves may be hidden from you at this time and you could feel a little at sea if you try to push yourself to hard. Use this period to discover your inner self by doing some meditation, yoga, journaling or simply having a think. Don't let angry feelings bottle up.

Friday 29 July

You will not impress anyone by only doing the jobs that are forced upon you. What's more, a certain degree of control over your own destiny is expected if you want to take the step up. Remember, the people who have earned their positions have done so by taking the tough decisions. You want more responsibility at work but are reluctant to stand up and accept the tough jobs.

Saturday 30 July

You are developing a 'reed bending in the wind' philosophy about work, which will have a great effect on your colleagues' perception of you. However, this philosophy may affect your ability to motivate and achieve goals. The pleasures of life are opening up to you more and more. Some pastimes that you were engaging in reluctantly, like going to the gym because you need to get fit, are becoming second nature.

Sunday 31 July
Remember that a nimble mind requires a healthy environment and a healthy body. So, neglecting your wellbeing and ignoring growing relationship problems will do nothing for your long-term goals. Find a balance and you will be better off than most. In your bid for mental excellence, you tend to focus on matters of the mind. This leads you to neglect aspects of your life that are less cerebral.

Monday 1 August
We may be living in a limited world of other people's making, which could be at the expense of our own happiness and growth. We must ask ourselves if we are in touch with our true nature. All too often we have simply gone along with the status quo, just thinking within the parameters that we have been told exist for a reason.

Tuesday 2 August
This is a great day for diplomacy, so if there is anything that you want to get out on the table, do it now. You will find that you and your partner are in the mood to see each other's point of view. As communicative forces are on your side, you might find that you are much more in touch with others and empathy comes easily.

Wednesday 3 August
Be prepared to visit a relative for nothing more than a chat and a coffee. Be sure to talk about work and give the impression of success, even if that is not quite the reality. You've been out of touch with your wider family for a while and the ramifications will surprise you. This

visit will also put you in the good books with those who chatter.

Thursday 4 August

Energies are more sensitive and thoughtful this evening and create good vibes between the sexes. Creative ventures entered into should be ready to peak right about now, with your efforts moving forward very quickly towards completion. Domestic and family life will take precedence, and your family will benefit from new insights or ideas regarding problems in this area. These may actually come from an outsider, but will be welcome nonetheless.

Friday 5 August

As the new Moon sets in the sky tonight, set your lunar goal high and don't be afraid of failing. Remember the little reed, bending to the force of the wind, soon stood upright when the storm passed over. Try taking on more than you think you can handle. You might surprise yourself with your strength under fire.

Saturday 6 August

Tensions can be caused by family members who assert a blood-thicker-than-water right of access for your time. This might involve emotional blackmail that makes you turn to other relatives for help. Commitments to your family or work mean that you have had less than enough time to give to your closest friends, who are at least smart enough to realise that you are not purposefully neglecting them.

Sunday 7 August

There is a link that goes back to childhood and you might find that your parents know more about this than anyone else. You are a little overzealous about working through issues affecting your subconscious. To those who prefer a more concrete reality, it seems you are too self-obsessed and unable to recognise what they see as real problems affecting their lives.

Monday 8 August

What you want is not about to happen without a struggle, so you should rely on your charisma to convince the masses. You want to see everything and everyone working together on something that you feel is very important. Part of the problem is that you are working with a whole set of differing philosophies and priorities. An unexpected event will work in your favour if your timing is good.

Tuesday 9 August

There is a feeling that contemporary thought wants to leave you behind, but you have to find your niche in a new way. The older you get the more you are aware that the burden of responsibility is on the shoulders of the new generation. Always willing to take on the lion's share, don't become embittered by the fact that your contribution to society is, or will become, less and less recognised.

Wednesday 10 August

Go to the park today, with or without the kids, and find a nice tree to sit under. There seems to be a lot of politics going on around you. Hopefully today you have dragged yourself away from the office gossip and TV long enough to ground yourself in simple pleasures. If you are not the meditative type, you might like to kick a ball around or take a country drive.

Thursday 11 August

While you have had your share of bad experiences in life, and this shows from time to time in your prejudices, you have every right to defend your emotional stability against excessive prying. Of course, there is a fine line between prying and caring. Be careful not to rebuke those who are concerned about your wellbeing. If you are open, people will not need to pry.

Friday 12 August

Exhibit flexibility and compassion or resign yourself to great tedium. The ability to take on new ideas and empathise with others will breed creativity. This will lead directly to new opportunities at work and strong new social bonds. Also, be ready with Plan B in case friends or business associates cancel at the last minute. Tonight, find an activity that lets you forget any frustration from the workday.

Saturday 13 August

The opportunity to develop new skills will present itself at work today. Make sure that you are in a suitable state to make the most of this new knowledge; it will count in your favour soon. You might be struck by the irony that you could do great things with your mind if you applied it, but then you wouldn't have so much time for happiness.

Sunday 14 August

The originality and fertility of your mind will be put to great use in your home and domestic life. However, successes of the intellect may be tempered by a touch of the absent-minded professor. You are inclined to take on too much responsibility for your parents and will become easily frustrated. For this reason, your judgment may not be as infallible as it appears to be.

Monday 15 August

At some point today your magnetic charm will get a shot of charisma infused with willpower. Compliments may fool you into thinking that you are master of all that you survey. Be aware that those around you have their own agendas; that you are as dependent upon them as they are upon you. A quick decision will go your way and you can accomplish tasks with originality, which may bring status.

Tuesday 16 August

You are entering a stage of life where you will need some sustenance when it comes to self-development. Something has got to give and you should tell someone about these pressures, so that you don't begin to crack. You may desire to increase your time at home and an opportunity to reinforce a strained relationship, but professional demands are leaving you exhausted and more than a little grumpy.

Wednesday 17 August

It's party time over the coming weeks as Venus enters your romance sector. This is a fabulous period for finding friendship and possibly even love, as your romantic sensibilities are heightened and you socialising is very attractive. Crafts and hobbies benefit, as do your relations with children. You are in the mood for fun and love, and when you are smiling, the whole world returns your grin.

Thursday 18 August

The white noise begins to clear and the lines of communication free up again as Mercury comes out of its backwards motion in your communications sector. This has been a bad time for the information-freak Gemini as the post got lost, emails went astray and the battery on your mobile seemed to be permanently on the blink. Misunderstandings will clear and be a thing of the past.

Friday 19 August

As the Moon rises like a silver coin in the sky tonight, check where you are on your lunar path. Are you in the position you should be or have you slipped? Remember that laziness begins in cobwebs and ends in iron chains. Don't allow inertia to take a hold, as it is much harder to build momentum from a standing start than from even the most sluggish pace.

Saturday 20 August

You believe in other people's intuition but sometimes doubt your own abilities. Your access to these powers is a matter of learning and developing your knowledge. Associating this prescience with clichéd descriptions is a simplistic defence and means that you won't take advantage of your opportunities. Open your vision of the world to include the power of the mind and you will encounter a signpost to even more information.

Sunday 21 August

Try to immerse yourself in current world affairs. Your fresh take on these issues will open new insights for those around you. You are able to remain objective to a certain degree, and you attract people for advice and counselling for this reason. It is a politically charged time and you will learn about yourself by observing what is happening in the newspapers.

Monday 22 August

You have been struggling to make gains in your career for some time now, but just as it seems you are getting noticed and your hard work is beginning to pay off, things seem to come to a standstill. Take heart, the harder you work now, the better your position will be to take advantage of this ground work in the future. If you fall on your face, you're still moving forward.

Tuesday 23 August

The Sun has entered your home sector and will remain there for the next month. You will find this a great time to spend with your family doing cosy stuff. This month is all about renewing your relationship with your children and parents. Keep your weekends free for inexpensive get-togethers. Make an effort to contact extended family, too.

Wednesday 24 August

It would be a mistake to assume that your inability to work in a team is proof that no one is of any use to you. You are keen to get things done, but no matter how useful other people are, you won't find it all that easy to take advantage of their well-intentioned offers. If there is someone who needs guidance, take a moment to point them in the right direction.

Thursday 25 August

Lead by example rather than push from behind. Someone is not too happy about the way you are treating them or dismissing things that they see as important. If this is a close friend or colleague, give them the respect you'd give someone else and take their arguments into consideration. Don't allow your fear to stand in the way of an understanding by imposing unrealistic constraints on behaviour.

Friday 26 August

You are gaining the sense that you may be falling behind the pack. If anything, this is a product of an inability to make decisions. You feel that most situations are not as clear-cut as everyone else seems to think. If you reassess things from someone else's point of view, you'll see how blinkered you have been; give people due credit for telling you how it is.

Saturday 27 August

You may be pleasantly surprised by forthcoming events this week; there is good news for you. It may relate to recreation or an invitation to take on a challenge, or a promotion or job offer. In family discussions, ensure that the point you're making contributes to the healing of the situation for all concerned. Remember that you could easily be on the receiving end of your own solution.

Sunday 28 August

You are almost at wit's end regarding ongoing issues in the work place. Ultimately, the frustration that goes with coordinating a group of people with different levels of dedication must be released in more constructive ways than increasing the tension by apportioning blame. If you are the boss, you might start kicking some heads to make people wake up. Be careful not to create a level of animosity.

Monday 29 August

Your health and fitness have taken a battering lately. Changing that pattern of behaviour has not been as successful recently, as it was in your younger years. You feel like the man who gave up drinking and smoking, and after a week of healthy living gave that up too. A motivational boost will come from an unexpected exercise buddy. This will give you the enthusiasm that you need.

Tuesday 30 August

A person's reputation is rarely in proportion with their virtue. Don't let yourself be unnecessarily intimidated. A bad dream will leave you disconcerted, but will also contain the key to a new perspective. The grandiose dreams and overly pompous attitudes that you have been experiencing in your social circle, and may have been hindering your relationships, have eased and you will find an ally in luck.

Wednesday 31 August

This is a time for status building, so call on some of your networking skills to get people organised. You will be able to push many projects forward by the strength of your conviction. This month will bring many career challenges for you, and it is time for your talents to come to the fore.

Thursday 1 September

Failing to support a partner in a family decision may be pivotal to romantic success this week. Above all, appear to be completely loyal; although the veneer of loyalty will backfire if you are not genuine. In order to make a good decision in your family life, you need to get beyond your emotions, and be the boss when it calls for it in your love life. Backing a partner on a decision could become critical.

Friday 2 September

Galileo wrote important works in popular Italian rather than the scholarly Latin. This set him at odds with parts of the establishment but made his work more accessible. Don't be afraid to make your messages clear and simple today. This approach will help you achieve the greatest effect with the widest possible audience. Your emotional stability should help you when communicating to others.

Saturday 3 September

A Moon is born in the sky tonight and with it the germ of an idea. Take it on with zest. Remember that adventure is not outside, it is within you. It has been said that there are two kinds of adventurers: those who go truly hoping to find adventure and those who go secretly hoping they won't. Perhaps this time you could truly hope you find it.

Sunday 4 September

As Pluto stops wandering slowly backwards through your relationship sector, you will find that the rather unreliable and changeable nature of this part of your life will settle down. At least, the surprises may still occur, but they are less likely to be unwanted. Take each challenge as it comes.

Monday 5 September

You may come up against people who are less career-minded than you, particularly in the work place. These people try to rationalise their belief systems with a devil-may-care approach to their logic. Lately you've felt strong of mind and today will be no exception, as your communication and people skills blend nicely. You'll be comfortable with your abilities, but don't take yourself too seriously – you can be sure others won't.

Tuesday 6 September

Once again you realise that only by controlling your own personal space, environment, thoughts and reactions can you make a difference, no matter how small or large. Work loads will require careful management if you are to maintain your balance. Take the time to order your responsibilities and your approach to their completion. Everything else will follow on from this structure.

Wednesday 7 September
When others are ready to sit down and talk reasonably, you'll be there for them, but while the hysterics continue, just sit quietly and concentrate on the space between their eyebrows. Small people will always try to belittle your ambitions. People of some greatness make you feel that you, too, can become great. Maintain the level of inspiration and focus that you have gained from their company.

Thursday 8 September
Find space to revisit old interests and you'll be pleasantly surprised at your latent skills and ability to develop in leaps and bounds. You may need to learn to say no to your friends, even though they badger you with the best intentions. You are allowing yourself to become distracted by material pursuits when you are all primed to take a big step in the development of your skills or spirituality.

Friday 9 September
You are generally feeling optimistic and will have a good day. However, there may be tension between your desire to gain materially and your desire to do what makes you happy. In this conflicted state you could make some risky investments. Try to fully consider and explore your motivations before making any commitments. With all this bubbling energy and optimism, your partner could find you quite demanding.

Saturday 10 September
On the work front, an unplanned development has put the rumour mill in motion. This stirs a number of emotions, but you are conscious of not allowing others to see the effect the situation has had on you. Chances are that these repressed feelings will re-emerge at home, which

will create some tension as your family will be forced to deal with any pent-up frustration you are experiencing.

Sunday 11 September
People will be spellbound by your 'charisma' and you will be able to motivate them to a cause or project easily. Don't be misled by all the hoopla. You may have mystified yourself as well as everyone else. Reassess the facts before attaching your name to a project. Later in the day, respond to a gesture in the spirit in which it was given.

Monday 12 September
Venus has put on her sensible shoes and entered your work sector. This means you will find beauty in the nitty-gritty details and you will have more patience for getting things done. Take advantage of this mood over the coming weeks by throwing yourself into work and signing off on any unfinished projects. Romance could blossom over the water cooler.

Tuesday 13 September
If you've learnt anything in your life, it's that you have to give everything a red-hot go. Use your confidence to lead the way as if all the luck in the world was yours – such confidence also unsettles your opponents. A strong will and courageous heart will be your greatest allies as you are forced into a situation that you have no experience dealing with.

Wednesday 14 September
Though your emotions are the strongest motivational factor in your behaviour, you are not inclined to wear your heart on your sleeve. You will find that your daily life will improve tremendously when you communicate your needs. While long-term trends in your life may not be going exactly the way you want them to, you certainly have plenty of short-term pleasures to enjoy – especially today.

Thursday 15 September

You find yourself living in the moment to make life enjoyable. This may create situations that have to be dealt with down the track. You have been born with an innate sense that life is meant to be a struggle, so when it is not, there is something wrong. Living right here and now with no plans and no recriminations is a skill for you to gain.

Friday 16 September

It seems that you have more than enough activity to keep you occupied as far as your social life is concerned. You might want to use your home as a place of entertainment this weekend, as this is an especially positive time to do so. If it needs a spot of redecorating, you are in the perfect frame of mind to make a good beginning.

Saturday 17 September

While you like people with a similar outlook on life, you also respect that your friends hold as tightly to their beliefs as you do. You will find yourself disagreeing with one or two of your friends about an issue that stirs your emotional embers. But remember that you didn't choose your friends for their tendency to agree with you, but for their intelligence and integrity.

Sunday 18 September

The full glory of the Moon can be seen in the sky tonight and with this plump juicy apple comes the zenith of your lunar goal. Don't let your rest come before your exertion. It is the definition of laziness to rest before you get tired. A Norwegian proverb says that the lazier a man is, the more he plans to do tomorrow. Act today.

Monday 19 September

Dealing with the truth gives you a sneak preview of some very real solutions to work problems. It may be a tough day at the office, but you'll come home with the feeling that you accomplished something and deserve to put up your feet a little. The best idea may be to bring dinner home with you, then everyone can relax.

Tuesday 20 September

The only way to get away from your situation is to make a decision to break free by doing something unique. Try a type of clothing that you have always wanted to wear, but never have. It can be so easy to fall into a drill – sleeping, eating, wearing and thinking the same thing and going about work the same way day after day. Looking forward to retirement is not much of a goal.

Wednesday 21 September

Your thoughts will be all fun and games over the coming weeks as Mercury enters your romance sector. This is your springtime, where your brain is on holiday and your conversation is all about hobbies and happy events. This is a great time to spend your days with children as they will be right on your level. Shows and musical performances are a great way to relax.

Thursday 22 September

It is important to take care of your mental and psychological wellbeing today and not force yourself into corners where emotional issues are concerned. Any negotiations that you get involved with today should be approached with caution. It is going to be more difficult than usual to make clear distinctions and decisions, so it is probably best to defer important judgements until you have a clearer view of the situation.

Friday 23 September

The Sun is highlighting your party sector this month and you will find yourself with renewed energy for your hobbies and social life. Make the most of your bright mood by spending time with your children and inviting friends over for a get-together. If you don't have kids, borrow someone else's! Your playful energy will make sure you all have a great time.

Saturday 24 September

You can criticise the past generation all you want but you are just repressing the obvious fact that you have your own weaknesses. You are repeating the mistakes of every person who harps on about 'the good old days'. No one's childhood was perfect, especially the teenage years. As you get older, try to live your own version of a good and positive existence.

Sunday 25 September

Your ideal trip may not go exactly as planned, so be flexible and adapt to new circumstances without chucking a wobbly. A train conductor, flight attendant or hotel receptionist might go way out of their way to make sure that you're comfortable. Sure, it's all part of the job – but rest assured, not everyone gets the royal treatment like you do.

Monday 26 September

You will experience a passing moment of clarity today, although it may not take the exact form that you expect. You have felt lately that something is holding you back, even if you haven't been able to pin point exactly what that is. There is a good chance that something will reveal itself today. You may find the real lesson if that block has been created from within, not without.

Tuesday 27 September

Everyone wants to change the world, but no one thinks of changing themselves. We all think we are doing OK and being as moral as we can be. Challenge yourself and you may discover a little grey in what did appear to be black and white. If you think nobody cares about you, try missing a couple of payments.

Wednesday 28 September

Take some time to plan something a little different with a cultural or educational edge, as this will round out your experience and leave everyone satisfied. Your mood is expansive today, so you will be keen to get among those you love to be with. As the day winds up, your place will be with a few of your oldest friends.

Thursday 29 September
Regrets can play on our minds for a long time. You need to recognise that you have done as much as anyone else over the years and the result is that you have a great deal of flexibility in your life. You should take the time to think about how fortunate you are to have good friends and family. With this stable base you will be able to pursue other interests.

Friday 30 September
There will be difficulties keeping your mind from wandering at work today, as you can't stop rehashing good conversations. You also have a number of demanding situations to conclude at work. You feel like you are meandering your way into a dead end. Don't take any of this stuff too seriously, as it will all resolve itself if you take the time to ask the questions and voice your fears.

Saturday 1 October
The more you believe in yourself, the more you build up momentum for positive events. In a manner of speaking, this is like manufacturing your own luck because the more prepared you are, the more you can take advantage of every opportunity. Get yourself up-to-date with current issues to discover what is happening around you and reassure yourself that your view is correct.

Sunday 2 October
Don't fall into the trap of believing everything people say, especially if you are being asked to make a financial commitment to a cause. Some people will have no qualms about bending the truth, particularly if it is bent in their direction. If you have the strength of conviction, you should be able to sort out fact from fiction. Look into things until you are satisfied that all is above board.

Monday 3 October

Hope is on the horizon as the new Moon climbs to heady heights. Remember that you can't cross the sea merely by standing and staring at the water. Even Moses had to walk. Don't indulge in vain wishes and stand by your decision to act, in whatever capacity and whichever way you care to. Right now, it doesn't matter what you decide to do, as long as you do something.

Tuesday 4 October

As Mars goes retrograde in the sector of your subconscious, you will find that your energy is lowered, although the outcome may not be fully apparent to you. You could even become angry or frustrated when you realise that someone behind the scenes is undermining your efforts. Expect to be a bit of a sleepyhead over the coming weeks.

Wednesday 5 October

Sometimes it seems that all you need to succeed is a cocktail of ignorance and confidence, and then success is almost assured. Every now and again you come across someone with a reputation for intelligence and understanding, and these people are the ones that inspire you. A person with lessons to teach you will cross your path today; be on the lookout.

Thursday 6 October

Your mind is, in computer speak, 'de-fragging'. This means that it's taking all the little bits of information that you have stored over the years and bringing them into a more ordered filing system for quicker and easier access. Today you will feel that your energy is free enough for you to get on with the job of growing wiser.

Friday 7 October

It may not be complete but there is one thing that's for sure – you can't write your autobiography posthumously. If you have doubts that there is anyone else out there bidding for the rights, you had better get to it. It's in your best interest to make wise decisions sooner instead of later, and don't be under the mistaken assumption that your story doesn't hold any value for anybody else.

Saturday 8 October

They say that two is company and three is a crowd, but there is a welcome third wheel to your relationship over the coming weeks as Venus enters your partnerships sector. This is a great time for reviving flagging relationships and reigniting the spark in long-term partnerships. You will find the idea of partnering very attractive, and it is a good time for taking an extra step in a romance, whether it be moving in together, marrying, starting a family or adopting a pet.

Sunday 9 October

Details and diligence are on your mind over the coming weeks as Mercury enters your work sector. You'll be thinking and talking about how you can make life easier for yourself and your colleagues. Make sure you back up all this talk with solid action. You could really make some of your tasks easier if you took the time to think about how you could go about them more efficiently.

Monday 10 October

You're active and ambitious, especially in business, and have an astute mind that allows you to work well. You should profit from your skills as much as anyone else. There is a chance that a colleague will be looking for a confrontation today. They would be better off choosing someone else, because today you are really on your metal, and not afraid to speak a few home truths.

Tuesday 11 October

If you devote yourself to something you love over the next few days, you will be relying on an understanding partner who probably hasn't seen you for a few days. The key is a certain understanding you have of the nature of the mind and each other's interests. You could subject your partner to possessiveness or jealousy in the next few weeks as your emotional commitment becomes more intense.

Wednesday 12 October

You are in for some serious rewards if you can pull your socks up and complete those tasks that have been left undone for some time. You have a strong sense of the proper way to live your life and you consider yourself an ethical being. You will begin to involve yourself in moral arguments with those you disagree with. Be careful on this front, as you could be treading on treacherous ground.

Thursday 13 October

What better way to vent your excess energy and frustration than on the sporting field. We all have our own tests of skill and ingenuity, and some people go about this in a completely different way to you. Seek to discuss this difference; you will be surprised by the insights you receive. The lesson could be dominated by a need to develop your creativity.

Friday 14 October

You have overextended yourself during a slow-moving spending spree and now that it has caught up with you, it has put your mind into a spin. If you are in a relationship, you will need to discuss this situation with your partner. You are inclined to act mysteriously in your relationships with the opposite sex, which results in unusual behaviour. Not the best approach under the circumstances.

Saturday 15 October

Sometimes you can be guilty of glossing over problems that you don't understand, or that require more than a little work on your behalf. One of your favourite responses is to go shopping. Retail therapy is fine to an extent, but you know that it is only addressing a symptom and the real problems continue to remain unresolved.

Sunday 16 October

You are moving into a phase of original thinking that will enable you to be independent and innovative. With a sense of drama that is expressed positively you will draw the necessary attention to your endeavours without experiencing other people's jealousy. Even so, someone else's praise for your efforts will make no difference to the job that has been done.

Monday 17 October

The Moon is plump and full in the sky reminding you to work on your lunar goal. Remember, it is useless doing everything efficiently if it doesn't need to be done at all, so consolidate your activities and do only what it essential. At any rate, leave the tasks that can remain until the end, no matter how enjoyable. This month, it is definitely a case of eating your vegies first.

Tuesday 18 October

You are constantly thinking of the spoils of success and this causes you to consider other people as pawns, obstacles or merely physical objects that you have to deal with in the course of your day. As you perfect the habit of dealing with people it will begin to influence your relationships with family and friends. Your relationship with your partner is built on an open interchange of feelings.

Wednesday 19 October

Bad news if you have a looming deadline for a creative project, as most artists work with the natural ebb and flow of impression and expression. Problems with lazy or incompetent co-workers could also hamper your progress. If you are going to get competitive, choose to do it with an old friend who doesn't mind a little blood-letting on the basketball court of life.

Thursday 20 October

Look forward to an approaching meeting at work with a smile and a positive frame of mind, as this could be a good day to argue convincingly and resolve difficult issues. Though there may be some obstacles in your way, you are confident that the universe will give you a helping hand and that alone will get you through.

Friday 21 October

You are at the end of a trying period and feel a drain on your energies. Getting your body going again with exercise can boost your confidence and encourage positive thinking. Exercise doesn't have to be a chore, it can be fun. Find a partner and choose a sport that neither of you are good at or have played before. You will kick-start your psyche just by running around.

Saturday 22 October

You woke up on the wrong side of the bed today. Your partner will find your pernickety mood quite amusing. You could react to this by getting your back up or laughing at yourself. Seeing the humour in the situation is a much healthier reaction, and will bring you and your partner together rather than force you apart.

Sunday 23 October

Try putting a freeze on your generosity and stick to an exchange of views. Being over generous with time and effort will leave you exhausted. Remember, consider all aspects of your health, including your emotional and spiritual wellbeing. Fluctuating moods could lead you to think you have something seriously wrong with you, when in fact it is only a case of mental and physical fatigue.

Monday 24 October

The Sun has moved into your work sector, so this month you will find yourself with renewed energy to get many of the jobs done that have been left incomplete for too long. Your industrious mood will mean that you will be able to really push through and tick off some things on your list both at work and in the home. Don't waste this time on details. Just move on the projects that have been really weighing on your mind.

Tuesday 25 October

Today you are feeling as though it is time to reorganise your life, and clear out the closets both spiritually and in the real world. Until now you believed that you had enough money to last the rest of your life, but you need to rethink your position. You will continue to meet your present needs, but will also start thinking about the practicalities of the future.

Wednesday 26 October

You may be having second thoughts about a plan or project that has been in action for some time. This is partly because you feel that you are being hedged in by your own expectations. The reasons why you were originally excited and involved no longer exist. It is time to re-evaluate your present needs and whether your involvement in this plan meets those needs.

Thursday 27 October

You may need to put some things on hold if you can't concentrate. It is a waste of time trying to apply yourself when you constantly daydream. Dedicate one day to yourself and you'll return to your tasks with greater focus. It's better to avoid anything too structured unless you can have a quick look and move on.

Friday 28 October

You usually prefer to do things your own way because the result is often much better, and you are starting to remember why you thought that in a situation concerning money. Endeavour to tie up the loose ends in financial agreements today, particularly those involving friends. You could be offered something tempting in the way of material goods, but it's not all that it seems.

Saturday 29 October

The friendships that you share in your outer social sphere are harmonious today. Over the next few days you will experience luck regarding an object that you thought you had lost or that you would like very much to have. This could relate to physical fitness or a comfort that you once held dear.

Sunday 30 October

Today, you will find the support you need to get a creative project up and going. Oddly, you are also susceptible to momentary loss of speech and an inability to find the right words. Other people will hopefully consider this failure in communication part of your temperament.

Monday 31 October

Relationships and interactions are on your mind over the coming weeks as Mercury enters your partnerships sector. How you maintain a relationship, whether it be business or personal, is under the microscope and you can expect to learn as much about yourself as you will about the people around you. You can also expect to be the intermediary when things get heated between friends.

Tuesday 1 November

You must be in your party prime because your repartee is witty and your appearance charming and charismatic. Don't forget that while you are dazzling rooms full of people you barely know, you also need to develop strong friendships that you can depend upon. In recognising the value of these bonds you will also recognise your value as a friend.

Wednesday 2 November

As the new Moon awakes and reminds us to set our lunar goal, tell yourself that the best way to maintain momentum is to constantly set greater goals, until the momentum can take care of itself. When setting your mark, push it one or two steps higher. The worst you could do is fall one or two steps short.

Thursday 3 November
Your somewhat overgenerous behaviour is likely to serve as a decoy to distract people from witnessing your hangups. Part of your self-image is built around your charitable nature, but this is not always respected, as people are cynical of those who give money to beggars to buy off their own conscience. Happiness comes from the new ideas of an international traveller.

Friday 4 November
You are getting used to all the attention you have received lately. When a huge force of goodwill is coursing through your veins, the accolades from your associates will be coming thick and fast. In the past, you might have found that some of your well-meaning advice missed its mark and that the uplifting feeling of doing good work was not there. If your motivation is to assist other people, you will do fine.

Saturday 5 November
Most people have no idea of the extent they can command when they focus all of their resources on mastering one thing. The biggest problem some of us face is that we spread our energies too thinly by trying to focus on too many projects at once. If you have a great deal of work on your plate, you may need to 'rationalise' the important projects.

Sunday 6 November
As Venus rises in your finance sector, you will find yourself attracted to the dark side in more ways than one. Keep an eye on your money as gambling and short-term loans become more appealing. Lovemaking will take on new meaning as the physical side to your relationship benefits from the warm rays of this planet. Religion also takes on

an attractive veil. Over the coming weeks, you will find joy in ruminating over the 'truth' of life.

Monday 7 November

Some people insist on going the long way around just because it's a well-worn path. Your partner is complaining that you are starting to take the easy path in your relationship and he could be right. Something has been stirring up your romantic situation long enough for you to have to deal with it constructively rather than just trust that your usual routine will stand you in good stead.

Tuesday 8 November

If you are going to invest, the surest bet is investing in yourself, for you can at least guarantee that no one will embezzle your capital. You have a sense of trepidation about your own abilities at the moment. You could be the strongest, wisest person in the world and still feel uncertain. You will feel most comfortable being close to your family with whom your emotional ties are very strong.

Wednesday 9 November

There are strong urges from the universe to peel your eyes back and see what is in front of you, not what you want to see or what you think should be there. Work, health, money and romance are all in advantageous positions. You are well aware that you are reaping the rewards of a mind thoroughly connected with your emotional state.

Thursday 10 November

You should be encouraged to think great thoughts, to consider broadening your horizons, or expanding your range through travel and discovery. Instinctively responsive to the needs of others, you usually adapt to different people and changing circumstances by finding ways to make yourself useful. This skill will prove invaluable in the not too distant future, and in any travel plans you may be hatching.

Friday 11 November

You think that some people consider you flighty, but this is merely a symptom of your imagination and creativity. If you catch a glimpse of sky, you are happy to take off. Although you have altruistic motives, you have a tendency to act the martyr when your counselling is ignored. It is not unheard of for you to use guilt as a weapon when you want to elicit the attention and cooperation of others.

Saturday 12 November

Whichever way you decide to lighten up your world or ambitions, it's sure to draw you plenty of favourable attention. This decision will allow you to move on with some issues that you know you should be taking care of in your relationship, but the common advice is to the contrary. Your sensitivity extends to others and you will find people respond well to your counsel today.

Sunday 13 November

You are able to remain objective to a great degree and people come to you for advice and counselling for this very reason. You could use this to your advantage, especially when deepening your relationship and working towards your goals and aspirations. This talent also allows you to see complex situations in a clear light.

Monday 14 November

Over the next few weeks you will be open to doing things you wouldn't normally try. You may become caught up in the excitement of buying a timesaving device, like a dishwasher, or something more pleasing like a new sofa or bed linen. This activity could easily become a distraction, though, and hardly a catalyst for change. Victories will be won through perseverance and an open attitude to change.

Tuesday 15 November

As Mercury starts its frustrating course backwards through your relationships sector, you may feel like all the gains you have made have come to nought. Communications will be very fuzzy between you and your partner at this time and you may not be able to get across exactly what you mean to say.

Wednesday 16 November

Take advantage of the bright light of the full Moon to kick along your lunar goal. They say that if you are not going forwards you are going backwards, which is a comfort for those going full pelt. Make sure you are going about things efficiently and not getting caught up in the little details. Now is the time to get the bulk of your work done. The spit and polish can wait until the end.

Thursday 17 November

Over the next few weeks you will feel that you have made good ground towards creating balance in your life. You will feel ready to take advantage of all opportunities that come your way. This is not to say that you should jump at the first dangling carrot that comes into view. Preferably, you will go out and create the opportunities that you are after.

Friday 18 November

If your self-confidence lets you down, you should be constantly looking for ways to improve your assertiveness. A great place to start is with your personal willpower, giving up habits or finishing work projects that should have been completed long ago. Also, you will have to remind someone close to you that procrastination is the art of keeping up with yesterday.

Saturday 19 November

All rules are out the window in your family life and it seems that to move forward things must degenerate into a terrible mess of spite. Sometimes you have to give up trying to solve a problem if others aren't putting in the effort. If you've made all the hard decisions about your health, they will begin to pay off.

Sunday 20 November

You are not above using your inability to achieve perfection as an excuse for your own idleness and unproductivity. Regroup and prepare for your next attempt to inspire yourself and force yourself out of your comfort zone. Good relationships with your partner are another offshoot. Giving your support and encouragement instead of criticism will make you both happier in the long and short term.

Monday 21 November

The planet of the bizarre and the unexpected, Uranus, is moving forwards again in your career sector. You may have felt like your wider social conscience was not in sync with others in this area of your life, but this time has come to an end. Interesting solutions to old problems will become available to you.

Tuesday 22 November

Mercury is rising in your education sector, so expect to be thinking and talking about all that you know over the coming weeks. A course that you have been interested in studying for a while may present itself, or you could get the opportunity to take a trip overseas. This time is all about expanding your horizons and talking in terms of the big picture rather than getting caught up in the annoying details.

Wednesday 23 November

Social concerns are on your mind and you may find yourself involved in some charitable work. You don't offer your services very often and may want to tell everyone about it, but keep a firm grip on your modesty. By deciding to act for your own benefit you have to admit to the shortcomings that led you to the decision.

Thursday 24 November

Saturn, the planet of discipline, has rapped you over the knuckles in your communications sector, and will frustrate you even more with the obstacles he creates. This part of your life will seem to weigh you down like a stone around your neck, but you only get strong neck muscles from exercising them.

Friday 25 November
Trust yourself to be interesting and humorous, since too much premeditation will unsettle the people you need to impress. Your thoughts are not invisible, but are worn on your face like a badge. If you are not confident within yourself, it will show, but everyone else has been in your position before. Beware of vanity and superficial behaviour, as you can be self-centred.

Saturday 26 November
There is a small argument waging between some of your oldest friends and you may be able to calm both sides. Take the time to talk to them individually and really listen to what they are saying. In the end, they'll figure it out on their own.

Sunday 27 November
This month you have been shining artistically and finding a lot of energy to create beautiful things. This energy could also be directed towards social causes. If you are inclined, see if you can work directly with people in need. Your romantic and relationship energy is already phenomenal, but it is just about to move to a higher level again.

Monday 28 November
A career aspiration or something to do with your status in the work place will receive a boost today. You will find yourself somewhat obsessed on the work front with minor victories in the hope they will translate into something major. On the flipside, things might get a little tense if you and your partner are unable to agree about the amount of effort required around the home.

Tuesday 29 November
This is a great week for putting yourself forward powerfully in your career. For decisions that require a prompt response and a good feel for the situation, you will be more than capable of meeting the test. If you are a politician or a teacher or you are active in social causes, this is your day to mobilise people with the force of your personality.

Wednesday 30 November
Try to explore your cultural interests by visiting a gallery or performance that takes your fancy. You will find you are provided with much fodder for consideration and conversation, which brings me to another point. You must have the last word in every conversation and, as far as you are concerned, your word is the only one that counts. Your friends and associates are tired of this behaviour.

Thursday 1 December
As the new Moon gently swings into action, excite yourself with the possibilities of this next lunar adventure. If you invest your heart in everything, you can grasp many adventures within this life. Where and what shall it be? Make your choice happily, because if you don't find anything pleasant, at least you shall find something new.

Friday 2 December
Use your instincts and intuition when making any decisions or considering changes to your daily life. It's a good day to put in place the necessary systems for your continued progress at work. There will be ample opportunity to be generous when someone is in great need. In the meantime, you can focus on your own requirements.

Saturday 3 December
Looking your best is a top priority for you lately, so anyone who has to compete with you for mirror time at the gym is probably out of luck. This focus on beauty will

bring a new admirer into the picture. If you're not interested, you need to say so directly, but don't think that gossip will cease altogether.

Sunday 4 December

With a critical eye for organisation and detail and a constant search for perfection, you have an irresistible urge to improve everything and everyone, whether they need it or not. This does not often meet with the welcoming smile that you expect. You believe that you are trying to help people, but are you really? You will find solace in close friends and familiar social situations.

Monday 5 December

Mercury is moving forwards again and communications will become clearer. This frustration was first in your relationship sector, but lately it has been felt in your work sector. Take heart, as of today, you should have no more problems. Well, at least for the next couple of weeks!

Tuesday 6 December

Your boss might notice you smiling dreamily one of these days, and it might not go down very well! Certainly, keep your eyes on the bigger picture but don't lose sight of all those trees in the meantime. You could easily have the masses in your hands today, but would you put them to good use or personal use? Don't confuse other people's needs with your personal objectives.

Wednesday 7 December

It can be difficult dealing with feelings of failure, but it is far worse never to have tried to succeed. You are feeling conflicted about changing your self-expression in a way that manages to maintain your sense of self and your role in this lifetime. Someone will want to spend some time with you and it would be good to keep things quite casual by seeing a movie or a band.

Thursday 8 December

You are in no mood for competitive people and no amount of pushing will raise a response. The beauty of a simple truth is your theme today, and you are enjoying musing upon the bigger questions in life. This will enable you to implement projects that have been sitting on the back burner for some time, the ones you truly hold dear.

Friday 9 December

You have been feeling very apathetic lately, especially in the sector of your subconscious, but that has eased now. Mars is moving freely again, and you can expect his powerful energy to really rev things up. Move on any projects you had in mind, particularly charitable works, such as working with the disadvantaged or disabled.

Saturday 10 December

Take satisfaction from what you do and attempt to enjoy it without seeking social confirmation. Your thoughts will turn to your material sector over the next year or so, and you could find yourself earning a lot more as your needs increase. You will be very fortunate if you love to work.

Sunday 11 December

Inner conflicts have been awoken by a chance encounter with an old associate. You were unaware that such ideas were harbouring in your psyche, and they will cause feelings of tension or possessiveness. Certain discoveries and personal revelations are on the way – welcome them. You are finding comfort in the home and your domestic security is taking top priority at the moment.

Monday 12 December

In your communication you will exhibit a variety of expression that others admire. Openness is not exactly your strong point, so it may be perceived that you are not taking things seriously. Look for quality in all things, even work that you don't like, as this will get you through a rough patch.

Tuesday 13 December

You've had a little bad luck lately and it seems that this tremor might escalate into an avalanche, but it will never be as bad as you first think. Sometimes you feel as though you are going backwards in your attempts to progress at work, but accept that advancement can be a slow process. This is not to suggest that you should hold yourself back for someone else's benefit.

Wednesday 14 December

You are not finding any consolation in people's hokey sayings today. You have a thirst for more meaningful answers. Yoga and meditation are good for you at this time as they block out the external intrusions and allow you to tap into the universal energy source, giving you added endurance and recuperative powers. Soon, you will meet those hokey sayings with a knowing smile and a warm glow.

Thursday 15 December

When the full Moon peeps over the horizon tonight, expect to have renewed energy for your lunar goal. According to the wisdom of the proverbs, the slug that does not plough after the season, begs during the harvest and has nothing. Make sure you are ploughing right now, so you will not be begging at the end of the lunar month.

Friday 16 December

As Venus sits down for a deep and meaningful in your education sector, you will find reading and schooling more appealing. An overseas trip could sound pretty good right now, and you are sure to find yourself in more than one art gallery or beautiful building if you are planning to travel over the coming weeks. If renovating, you may have the impulse to decorate with objects from different cultures. An exotic bird could capture your heart.

Saturday 17 December

Grand gestures define your relationships with most people and perhaps it is time to pull one of those finer moments out of your bag of tricks. If you are in the mood for romance, splurge on someone you love and entertain the idea of an impromptu meal out. You're a friend's best source for support right now, because your strength comes from your emotional independence.

Sunday 18 December

Do you have that sinking feeling that you are becoming more of a passenger in life than an agent of real change? You can have more of an impact at this time by making certain your actions aren't contributing to petty power plays or manipulative dealings. You will find yourself behaving in a stubborn and impervious manner to changes not of your own making.

Monday 19 December

Prudent is not a word that will appeal to your state of mind right now, but it is one that will fare you well if taken seriously. You are in your element at work and finding a lot of comfort from the daily grind. By making well-informed decisions, and not jumping at the first opportunity that comes your way, you will make great advances in the near future.

Tuesday 20 December

You will be forced to bring all of your mental energies to a particular problem in order to reap rewards. Your creative resourcefulness will allow you to dig deep to find the elusive solution. Don't be surprised if you are forced to turn to others for advice. If the problem is of a personal nature, consult your parents, as you will be impressed with their response.

Wednesday 21 December

You should tread very carefully because you don't want to damage your relationships with a plea for space that is interpreted as a demand to 'back off'. Be careful not to let your emotions distract you from making difficult decisions, and communicate your thoughts in an open yet considerate way with your partner and friends.

Thursday 22 December

Today the Sun moves into your financial sector, so tie up any loose ends and get those loans paid off that have been hanging around your neck. This is also a period when you'll find yourself questioning your long-held beliefs and testing your faith a little. This is an excellent time to renew commitments and refresh stagnant relationships.

Friday 23 December

The world has been motoring along a very conservative path for a couple of months now, and this has been particularly frustrating for forward thinkers like yourself. You are keenly aware that individual needs must sometimes be sacrificed for the common good, but don't become a doormat for other people. It is this self-sacrificing attitude that will get you noticed for a promotion in the future.

Saturday 24 December

You would do well to start valuing your time, which is impossible if you don't value yourself. Your lesson is to work out what you really need to achieve and what is mere window dressing. Other people's hearts skip a beat when they consider the talent you are letting slip away. It is time to stand up and be accountable for what you are capable of.

Sunday 25 December

A festive day for most, today is not without some frustrations, as Venus decides it is time to charge backwards through social sector into career sector. You may not be able to charm your audience as you would like, and you may find that your natural ability to woo your way into what you want is not available to you.

Monday 26 December

The grandiose dreams and overly pompous attitude that you have been accused of in your relationship are easing and you will find an ally in communication. You have to let people know what your emotions are if they are to help you along the way, and don't deny that you need some help either. The more you draw people out, including your partner, the easier it will be to find compromises.

Tuesday 27 December

You are faced with the problem of motivating a group towards a common goal, one that you may not believe in yourself. Some people will know your type and be too intelligent to succumb to inspiring words or cheap bribes. Attempt to be as honest as possible with everyone involved. Keep an eye out for what's really going on around you before you place blame.

Wednesday 28 December

If a close relative or family member keeps contradicting themselves, just sit back and watch the situation develop instead of trying to intervene. You will never divine what it is that they're trying to accomplish or want you to do. This may well create all sorts of problems because you are not always receptive to cries for help when others become a little fed up or frustrated with you.

Thursday 29 December

Ideas and projects seem to dominate your waking hours. You find yourself juggling each idea as it springs into your mind, trying to find a way to put them all into practice. If you've been promising to do certain things, even if you can't stomach the thought of them, these should be the first cabs of the rank. If you live up to your word, your credibility will be enhanced.

Friday 30 December

You will appear to take a submissive stance on matters, which is just a front while you choose the best time to make your moves. You are often questioned because of the way that you go about things. You can understand the concerns of your friends, but you are happy with this method of operation. This makes you sensitive to the difficulties of others, which is very much appreciated.

Saturday 31 December

The end of the year brings a beginning in the shape of a new Moon. Take some time out from the festivities to reflect on what 2005 has taught you and commit to your next lunar goal accordingly. Allow yourself to enjoy what you have achieved over the past year. You have come a long way, baby!

THE GEMINI
SUN SIGN

THE GEMINI CHARACTER
(22 May to 22 June)

*'I'm a very natural flirt, but I don't see it in a sexual way
. . . a lot of the time I'm like an overexcited puppy. I think
I'm being friendly with someone, they think I'm flirting with
them.'*

Kylie Minogue (singer),
Gemini sun sign, born 28 May 1968

BASIC CHARACTERISTICS OF THE SIGN

Personal creed – I think

Positive/masculine sign

Element – Air

Energy – Mutable

Psychological type – Thinking

Glyph – ♊ The two lines represent the two children, the
two bright stars, Castor and Pollux of classical
mythology

Colours – Yellow, blue

Body parts – Hands, breath

Metals – Mercury, alloy, mercury compounds

Gemstone – Agate

Flowers – Azalea, lavender, lilac, lily of the valley, myrtle,
sweet pea

Trees – Nut-producing trees

Food – Salads, fruit, fish

People with a Gemini sun sign are generally:
- Witty
- Lively

- Inquisitive
- Sociable
- Agile
- Teasing

On the other hand, they can also be:
- Nervy
- Superficial
- Inconsistent
- Cunning

Geminis love:
- Variety
- Multi-tasking
- Flirting
- Fun
- Telling stories

But they can't stand:
- Boring people
- Overly emotional behaviour
- Possessiveness
- Jealousy

SOCIALLY

Gemini is most happy when they are socialising. It is their life's work. They make an art out of being at ease in a social situation, mingling and moving around the room, making sure they can extract as much information as they can in the shortest period possible.

The Gemini metabolism is generally too quick to get them in too much trouble with alcohol. That said, they like to have a glass in their hands at all times. If the party is really pumping, you will know because Gemini will still be toting around the same warm glass of flat champagne at the end of the night, because they have been far too busy to stop and drink up. If the party has been a real flop you will know because Gemini will be back at the bar every ten minutes, ordering another strange cocktail, usually with a theme in mind. Geminis get bored rather quickly and they can be a bit like a canary in a mineshaft when it comes to judging your party's success.

RELATIONSHIPS

'Husbands are chiefly good as lovers when they are betraying their wives.'

Marilyn Monroe (actress),
Gemini sun sign, born 1 June 1926

You probably met your Gemini friend at a party, looking completely at ease, playing the room with a drink in one hand and a cigarette in the other. She was flitting from group to group, leaving them laughing, and then moving on effortlessly to the next huddle.

It was a surprise, then, to discover she didn't actually know the host. She was there with a friend: 'He's over there,' she said, waving her hand airily in no particular direction. Her bright and expressive eyes remained locked on yours.

You think you might be falling in love. Who is this witty little lady? But before you know it, she is gone. The only thing left is the invigorating smell of lavender and her glass of champagne, left on the sideboard and barely touched. You realise it will take a little more than the ordinary to captivate the attention of this rare bird.

Geminis make fickle lovers. You can be in the middle of a passionate embrace when something catches their interest out of the corner of their eye. It might be a book on the desk, or a picture on the wall, but they will make a comment and expect you to answer in a logical, conversational manner. If you do manage to gurgle out an answer, the lovemaking will resume. For a Gemini, this is par for the course, but for others it can be a real candle-snuffer.

Geminis use sex as they use most activities – to avoid boredom. Their penchant for variety and constant stimulation often finds Gemini with the strangest bedfellows. The greatest aphrodisiac for a Twin is a partner with a flashing wit. What the Gemini most craves is not the physical affection that comes from making love, but the verbal run-up to it. Sometimes the flirting is much more satisfying for the Gemini than the consummation of lust. They love talking themselves into, and then back out of, bed with all sorts of people.

CAREER AND MONEY

'The ignorance of one voter in a democracy impairs the security of all.'

John F Kennedy (US president),
Gemini sun sign, born 29 May 1917

People enjoy working with Geminis for their cheery natures and funny one-liners. They can be an important lynchpin in the social fabric of the office and are also keepers of the office gossip.

With Mercury ruling, Geminis make wonderful salespeople or journalists, but they could also find themselves in more manual jobs, like carpentry, lead-lighting, ceramics, jewellery or textiles, as they find working with their hands almost meditative. They also make very quick typists. They can be very expressive while talking, and their gesticulations can seem to take on a life of their own. They have a talent for magic tricks. With their ability to communicate, Geminis make engaging teachers, especially of high-school students, who find them nonpatronising and easy to relate to.

Gemini's anchor is words. They find a sense of safety in talking and exercising their excellent memories. They often have conversations in their heads. They also have a habit of absorbing information and instantly converting it into their own words in their minds. A Gemini will read, collate, simplify and imagine telling someone about it all at the same time. Some people are content to learn for their own sake. A Gemini learns for the joy of relaying the information onto others.

Geminis like to be able to verbalise everything. Of course, some emotions can't be put into words, and a Gemini will struggle with these, and eventually seem to lay them to one side. This filtering of emotions through the intellect can come across as calculating or aloof.

With all these abundant talents and charms, people are incredulous when they find out that Geminis have very little faith in themselves. Often it will be masked with an ironic wit or sarcasm. A Gemini would rather not do something at all and be thought of as unreliable, than do it badly and be thought of as incompetent or stupid.

This means Geminis are not good at pushing themselves into new projects. They have the verbal skills to mask any gaps in knowledge, and people can be enthralled by their insights, but their fear of looking stupid holds them back from making big breakthroughs. This is a huge pity, as the Gemini's flexible mind would be valuable in upper-management roles.

Geminis see money more as a tool in itself than a commodity to be collected. This healthy attitude means that they rarely get hung up about debts owed to them, and equally debts that they owe themselves. They are quick of mind and tongue and therefore have no trouble attracting money, but they are rarely interested in holding onto it for too long.

Gemini is a yang sign, that is, a positive, masculine energy force, but the symbol of the Twins tells us there is more to the story. The Twins are both yin and yang, which we all possess to varying degrees, but in Gemini it is extremely pronounced. In regards to money, this means that one hand can be taking it while the other is giving it away.

FAMOUS GEMINI SUN SIGNS

22 May 1813 – Richard Wagner (composer)
22 May 1859 – Arthur Conan Doyle (writer)
22 May 1907 – Laurence Olivier (actor)

22 May 1959 – Morrissey (singer)

23 May 1974 – Jewel (singer)

24 May 1819 – Queen Victoria (British royalty)

24 May 1941 – Bob Dylan (singer)

25 May 1963 – Mike Myers (actor/comedian)

26 May 1867 – Mary Queen of Scots (Scottish royalty)

27 May 1878 – Isadora Duncan (dancer)

27 May 1923 – Henry Kissinger (statesman)

28 May 1944 – Gladys Knight (singer)

28 May 1968 – Kylie Minogue (singer)

29 May 1903 – Bob Hope (comedian)

29 May 1917 – John F Kennedy (US president)

30 May 1474 – Albrecht Dürer (artist)

30 May 1908 – Mel Blanc (cartoons voice)

31 May 1923 – Prince Rainier III (Monaco royalty)

31 May 1930 – Clint Eastwood (actor)

1 June 1926 – Andy Griffith (actor)

1 June 1926 – Marilyn Monroe (actress)

1 June 1934 – Pat Boone (singer)

2 June 1840 – Thomas Hardy (writer)

2 June 1965 – Steve and Mark Waugh (cricketers)

3 June 1925 – Tony Curtis (actor)

3 June 1926 – Allen Ginsberg (poet)

4 June 1975 – Angelina Jolie (actress)

5 June 1956 – Kenny G (musician)

6 June 1955 – Sandra Bernhard (comedian)

7 June 1848 – Paul Gauguin (artist)

7 June 1940 – Tom Jones (singer)

7 June 1952 – Liam Neeson (actor)

7 June 1958 – Prince (musician)

8 June 1933 – Joan Rivers (comedian)

8 June 1940 – Nancy Sinatra (singer)

8 June 1955 – Tim Berners-Lee (inventor)

9 June 1893 – Cole Porter (songwriter)

9 June 1963 – Johnny Depp (actor)

10 June 1922 – Judy Garland (actress/singer)

11 June 1910 – Jacques Yves Cousteau (ocean explorer)

11 June 1934 – Gene Wilder (actor)

12 June 1929 – Anne Frank (writer)
13 June 1865 – WB Yeats (poet)
14 June 1811 – Harriet Beecher Stowe (writer)
14 June 1946 – Donald Trump (entrepreneur)
14 June 1961 – Boy George (musician)
14 June 1969 – Steffi Graf (tennis champion)
15 June 1954 – Jim Belushi (actor)
17 June 1867 – Henry Lawson (poet)
17 June 1878 – MC Escher (artist)
17 June 1882 – Igor Stravinsky (composer)
17 June 1917 – Dean Martin (singer)
17 June 1946 – Barry Manilow (singer)
18 June 1942 – Paul McCartney (musician)
18 June 1952 – Isabella Rosselini (actress)
19 June 1896 – Wallis Simpson (almost royalty)
19 June 1947 – Salman Rushdie (writer)
20 June 1909 – Errol Flynn (actor)
20 June 1972 – Nicole Kidman (actress)
21 June 1905 – Jean-Paul Sartre (philosopher)
21 June 1921 – Jane Russell (actress)
21 June 1973 – Juliette Lewis (actress)
21 June 1982 – Prince William (British royalty)
22 June 1936 – Kris Kristofferson (singer/actor)
22 June 1949 – Meryl Streep (actress)

SUN SIGN COMPATIBILITY

Have you ever wondered why people get together? Why some people fight like cats and dogs but stay passionately in love until the end of their days, while another couple might seem like the perfect pairing but finally divorce after years of unhappiness? Why some partners are as alike as brother and sister, and others are as different as a fish and a bicycle? What is the glue that sticks people together?

In the 1970s, it was considered a pick-up line if you asked someone, 'What's your sign?' It showed you were trying to get an idea of what that person was *really* like. Of course, no one can tell what you are really like just from your sun sign, but it is a good way of drawing people out to talk about what they think they might be like, which, I think you will agree, is just as instructive!

ARIES/GEMINI

A wonderful alliance. This is an exciting, sexual encounter that (dare I say it, because neither of you like to think too long-term) can last! Both Aries and Gemini are so spontaneous and full of life that there is no time for either of you to become bored. Intellectually, it will be a stimulating time as well.

However, this is a matching that is in danger of becoming superficial. Remember that love is a verb, a 'doing' word, and it needs to be expressed to exist. Both of these signs can be superficial but for different reasons.

Aries is inherently independent. They have trouble thinking of themselves as a couple, and will often thoughtlessly do something on their own that should be shared (like arranging your wedding!). This is not because they don't want to spend time with the other person and don't value their assistance, it is just that they are so used to doing things by themselves and in their own way.

Gemini's eloquent speech belies what they are thinking, as the Gemini mind is able to do the two things independently. You might think you having a deep and meaningful discussion about the possibility of having your first child, and certainly half of Gemini is there with you, but the other half is organising the guest list for the office Christmas party.

Aries is a straightforward sort of a person. If Aries is in a good mood, it will last for a while and he will do nothing to hide the fact that he is feeling good. Gemini can be exalted one minute and thoroughly depressed the next, behaviour that leaves Aries in a state of confusion.

Aries' response to Gemini's knockout beauty will flatter Gemini, but Aries operates on a search and conquer quest when looking for a partner and tends to quickly gain the upper hand if possible. Rebellious Gemini may find this too much of a temptation to revolt. Gemini should know that

Aries just likes to appear to be the decision-maker, and wily Gemini will always have her way if she is smart (which of course she is), she just has to keep Aries thinking he is the boss. In this way a wily old tom cat like Warren Beatty (Aries) can be subdued by a Gemini like Annette Bening.

Gemini needs fun, laughter and mental stimulation; routine is death to them and in this way you are perfectly matched. Flashes of bickering will characterise your communication, but neither has the desire to hold grudges for too long, although impish Gemini may have the laugh last by setting a trick, long after Aries has forgotten the fight.

The Social Aries

Aries can be a fickle party guest. Don't ever expect them to RSVP. In fact, the only confirmation you'll get is when they give you a call to ask: 'Is it OK if I bring Juan, my Brazilian drinking partner?' And don't be surprised if after acquiescing, they don't turn up anyway. With an Aries, you just never know.

In anyone else, this arrogant behaviour would be mildly infuriating, but in an Aries, you can't help but be bowled over by their puppy-dog enthusiasm. You can guarantee only one thing with an Aries – if they do turn up, they are not likely to be hanging off your coat-tails, waiting for an introduction. You rarely have to worry if Aries is having a good time. Aries brings the good time with them, they don't need anyone else to make things happen. If the conversation really isn't rocking their world, you might find them climbing the tree in your back yard, or clearing a space in the living room for a karoake competition.

Enticing them to come to your party in the first place is one thing, getting them out the door at the end of the night is another altogether. Aries are competitive about everything they do and that includes partying, so they want to make sure they squeeze out every last drop of fun before leaving. They are not particularly good at reading the moods of other party-goers either, and while everyone else is winding down, finding their coat and thinking about bed, Aries will be the one to find the last bottle of spirits and call everyone together for a limbo drinking competition.

They can be wildly flirty, especially if you seem a little hard-to-get. They are always up for a challenge but let that be a warning. Once they have won their prize, they might not be so interested in sustaining the passion.

They will do and say ridiculous things when tipsy, but they will expect you not to hold it against them. They are not materialistic and not big on predicting consequences, so they will find it difficult to understand your concern about the imported Greek rug they are proposing to have their limbo drinking competition on. And, when the inevitable does happen and black sambuca is trailed like tar across your irreplaceable floor covering, Aries will be charming and apologetic and will consider that the end of the story. Aries don't hold grudges unless they have been badly burnt, so they will be surprised when you maintain your indignation over something they consider pretty minor in the Universal scheme of things.

If you are invited to an Aries party, be mindful that the invitation could be the best thing about the party. Aries are great instigators and are fabulously creative while you have their attention, but by the time it gets to the big day, they may have run out of steam. A limp sausage in a bit of bread and a luke-warm lemonade could be the extent of their planned hospitality. That's not to say you won't have a great time, because the Aries personality has enough va-voom to get any wet squib of a gathering going, just don't go hungry or empty-handed.

How to Woo Your Aries

Fancy à la carte dinners are not the way to impress an Aries, as they usually regard food as more a necessity than a lavish gesture. Indulge his eclectic brain in a myriad of new experiences – take him salsa dancing, for a picnic at the zoo, to a smoky jazz club one night and to a Hare Krishna restaurant the next.

Keep the conversation lively, and engage him with a few witty anecdotes, but mostly let the flow revolve around him. It's usually a fine balance between being interesting and having your own opinions, and feeding his fire-eating ego.

Like a toddler, Aries mostly likes to play side-by-side rather than interacting and cooperating, and he will appreciate you having your own talents and hobbies rather than wanting him to be involved in everything you do.

When things get a little more smoochy, give your Aries a head massage or play with his hair and watch him melt like butter in your hands!

Gifts for Your Aries

Aries don't value possessions that much and can appear to be quite monastic in their preferred environment, so don't go to too much effort or expense. You will only be hurt when you find the expensive ring that you spent a week's wages on lying carelessly next to the plughole in the bathroom. And don't expect her to be too distressed when you tell her where you found it – she'll just be happy that you did!

More bookish Aries will love books on philosophy and ideas. Practical gifts like a Swiss Army pocket knife will be appreciated, as Aries value functionality. Music CDs are a good idea, and don't be too worried that you might not pick her taste; she will enjoy the new experience of something a little offbeat.

TAURUS/GEMINI

Taurus may find holding onto the flighty Gemini like holding onto a handful of dry sand. Geminis don't like to sit down mentally for one minute, while Taurus loves to muse.

The restless Gemini lives in a cerebral world of ideas and Taurus is very much based in the material. Also, the great sex drive of the earth sign might find little comfort in the Gemini take-it-or-leave-it approach to romance.

Gemini loves change and Taurus resists it, so this could be a major issue.

Taureans are romantics who play with a straight bat. They love to be wined and dined and enjoy a surprise, but they do not think secrets and mystery are particularly romantic like some of the other signs. Never try to hide something from a Taurus, even if you think that it is a little romantic to do so, because you are more than likely to upset them with your opaque ways. Taureans believe honesty and trust go hand in hand and will become annoyed if you expect them to trust you after you have appeared to be dishonest.

A straight bat does not mean straightlaced. Never assume for a moment that Taurus is as straight as she appears, for she often has interests that border on the eccentric. Collecting snow domes, playing the zither or translating the Bible from the original Hebrew are examples of some Taurus hobbies. You would probably never suspect they had these skills, except for their annoying habit of making gifts of their wares!

They are also very loyal. This can sometimes develop into possessiveness, and they should be aware that a life partner is not just a pretty addition to their homewares and manchester collection. A life partner cannot be so easily changed either. This can be a disappointment to the Taurus who, some time in the past, pulled a 'pre-loved' partner out of the bottom of the pile with the intention of sanding him back and polishing him up, but learned this is not so easy. The tenacious Taurus probably kept polishing long after the oak turned out to be nothing more than veneer on chipboard, tried to turn it into shabby chic and eventually gave up.

When he does find Mrs Right, the Taurus holds onto that beauty for dear life, sometimes to the point of smothering the loved one. However, Taureans make wonderful, sensuous lovers and can turn any shack into a home, so the object of his affection is probably not going to mind a little of the green-eyed monster, as long as it is kept in hand.

There are many who make it through. The Queen (Taurus) and Prince Philip (Gemini) are one example. Champion tennis players Andre Agassi (Taurus) and Steffi Graf (Gemini) have the sort of lifestyle that suits this pairing. The retired Graf provides the stability of a solid relationship by caring for their children, which is important for the Taurean Agassi. Agassi takes his family all over the world to compete in tournaments and provides Gemini Graf with the stimulation and excitement that she needs.

The Social Taurus

In general, Taureans can be quite a moderate sort in most areas of their lives. They don't like taking flashy risks and they don't go out of their way to make bolshy conversation. Generally, Taureans like to keep things going at a steady pace, straight down the middle, with few deviations.

That's not entirely true when it comes to drinking and dining. Taureans live for their senses to be stimulated and they are always looking for more delicious ways to feed their soul. So, although the social side to any party might be a plus, it is the sheer indulgence of well-made apertifs and hors d'oevres that will keep your Taurean in seventh heaven. Make sure you have a well-planned menu for your Taurus friend, something that reaches across all tastes. They will be looking for sweet, salty and sour flavours, something a little spicy hot, and something cool and refreshing.

After that, your party will be a cinch, because once a Taurus is sated, they have wonderfully warm personalities that keep the conversation roaring throughout the night. Some Taureans can be a little retiring except in close company, but others are conversation connoisseurs who know how to keep everyone entertained. Taurus prefers to drink at a leisurely pace, but as stated, they are not moderates when it comes to food or anything sensual, so if the booze is top quality, it might get a little messy. There is not a lot you can do about this. Keep their water glass topped up and they will thank you in the morning, but try to quash their quaffing and you could be heading for a confrontation, and no one wants to confront a Bull if they can help it.

That goes for late-night table-thumping stoushes, too. It is a brave person who disagrees with a Taurus, especially after a few vinos. Taureans uphold a veneer of fairness in their everyday lives that may lead you to believe that they are very open-minded and can see the subtle shades of grey in any political carpet. This is probably not the case. Most Taureans hold their views with an iron-fist and the sort of staunch stoicism only seen in unionists and the elderly. Fortunately, most Bulls have to be thoroughly provoked into entering the fray, but there are the odd Bulls that enjoy some discursive gymnastics as a round-up to any fine evening.

Expect any Taurean party to be a wonderfully lavish affair where everything hangs together beautifully. Like Librans, Taureans have a knack for bringing together the simplest of ingredients and making them work in a harmonious manner. The décor will be mellow and easy on the eye, the food exquisite and the beverages mouth-watering, no matter what budget the Taurus is working under.

How to Woo Your Taurus

Spoil your Taurus. No amount of money is too extravagant. Be sure to make some physical contact, touch his arm, look deeply into his eyes when you speak to him, ground him in your adoration. Physically and materially you must devote yourself to the Bull.

The Taurus enjoys good manners, and the female Taurus won't mind if you open the door for her or pull out the chair. Choose a good Italian restaurant for the first date (her favourite dessert is bound to be tiramisu). Do some homework as well, for she'll be impressed if you seem to know your way around a wine list. Feel free to order a good wine, after you know what she is eating, but don't order the dish for her. She is not that old-fashioned, and she always knows exactly what she wants to eat.

Dress nicely, smell good, clean your fingernails and use mouthwash. Flowers are a good idea, but only if you are picking her up from her place and she can arrange them before you go, as she won't gladly carry them around with her.

Gifts for Your Taurus

Anything that is particularly sensual and pretty to look at will be appreciated, especially if it will contribute to his comfort. A soft wool rug in a luxurious colour (make sure it suits the decor), lambskin pillow undercovers or an electric blanket are nice ideas.

Scented body creams and luxury beauty items are also a good idea. Most earth signs love moisturisers and will be obsessive about moisturising one part of their body, be it lips, hands or elbows. Decadent foodstuffs are always a treat. Look for exotic treats, such as pears preserved in creme de menthe, baklava or halva.

Jewellery and lingerie will be genuinely appreciated, but don't think that you can skimp on quality. Your Taurus knows intimately the difference between white gold and platinum, llama and alpaca, cotton and linen, red and black caviar. It's his life's work and he cannot be fooled.

GEMINI/GEMINI

Same-sign relationships are always a little trying. You appear to be perfect for one another, but can find yourself irritated by each other's predictability and faults. It is very easy to loathe in others what you dislike in your self.

This can be the major difficulty in same sun-sign partnerships. Your similarities ensure that you are always on the same wavelength. But it can almost be like seeing yourself through other people's eyes. It is a truism to say that you can't stand in others what you see in yourself, especially when you can't admit to it. Little habits and foibles that you never knew you had can come to light, and make you shudder with repulsion.

The other problem (which is in a similar vein) is seeing things in someone else that you have already struggled with and overcome. Surprisingly, having been through the experience doesn't always make you more forgiving of those with the same problem. Sometimes it will actually make you less empathetic.

One trait that is likely to get under your skin is the 'half-there' look that Gemini often gets in conversation, especially about matters of commitment. Both of you will be able to tell better than anyone when you are not really listening – this can be most annoying. You are also both likely to over-commit to social engagements and end up fighting over which party should take precedence. These are all small things that you can either bicker over till your dying days – or make a self-deprecatory joke, have a quiet smile to yourself and get on with your relationship.

John F Kennedy and Marilyn Monroe were both Geminis. Fleeting couple actor Nicole Kidman and singer Lenny Kravitz are also Geminis.

The Social Gemini

Flirting is always the issue with Geminis, and even the most married Gemini will have every man in the room thinking they might be in with a chance. It is their eagerness to please that often gets them into trouble, but it is their quick wit that will often get them out of any potentially nasty situation with everyone's egos in tact.

Should they decide to get really sloshed, their natural exuberance and social savvy means that their behaviour doesn't change that much. Be aware that your Gemini drinking partner may be fine one minute and horizontal the next, without appropriate warning.

A Gemini truly disgracing herself is not a regular occurrence, so often the only thing that is broken is a heel from one of Gem's tottering party shoes. (Geminis are usually a little shorter than the norm, but they like to make up for it by being taller in personality and in footwear.) Along the way, however, Gemini may have broken a few hearts.

See, Geminis love to play the room. They have been known to have most members of the opposite sex mentally picturing the children they will one day have together, but over the course of the evening, Gemini will let those individuals down gently so there are no hard feelings. If that evening is cut short by unforseen inebriation, Gem may not have had a chance to complete the flirtational cycle, and there may be some sweet alking to be done the next day. Worse still, someone may take it upon themselves to take advantage of the situation, so if you do see your Gemini friend looking a little wobbly at the knees, keep a close guard.

How to Woo Your Gemini

You won't find a Gemini on the dance floor or at the buffet; they will be at the bar, with every intention of buying a drink, just as soon as they talk to so-and-so. Geminis love a good chat and they love a sparkling mind even more, so just sidle up and say hello. They are one of the few signs to actually enjoy a good pick-up line, as long as it is funny or clever.

But that is as far as your proactive flirtation should go. When attempting to woo a Gemini, prepare to play woo-ee rather than woo-er. These guys know all the tricks in the book. In fact, they wrote the book, so don't try and beat them at their own game. They will be quite happy to take the lead.

Geminis love to be touched on the hands and arms, and are especially sensitive in these areas. A Gemini woman will enjoy having her hand kissed in greeting, for it allows her to look coquettishly through her eyelashes and also show off her lovely fingers.

Going to see a film with coffee afterwards at a nice café is a good idea for a first date. Geminis will love having a common learning experience like a film to talk about.

Gifts for Your Gemini

Books, music, videos or anything that will quench the Gemini desire for knowledge will be appreciated, as will theatre or concert tickets or an excursion to somewhere fun. Practicality and beauty are not your prime concern. You are looking for something that you can discuss and that will stir the mental juices. You can find the most remarkable things in electronic stores, or stores that sells puzzles and games.

Anything that keeps the hands busy, such as worry beads, will be well used. Geminis can't sit still for a moment and will love something that they can create while watching TV, such as tapestry or modelling clay. They also love to be as contactable as possible and will enjoy the latest mobile phones with all the trimmings, camera, mp3 player, Internet access and global positioning system. Tiny radios and TV wrist watches are also fabulous for Geminis.

Creativity and a sense of fun will impress more than expense and quality brand names, so think about something with a bit of novelty value; if it has a little story to go with it, all the better. They will love telling their friends about the funny gift you gave them.

CANCER/GEMINI

Warning, warning. Danger, danger. That scathing wit of Gemini's will cut the little Crab to the quick. Gemini has no patience for Cancer's moods, and the first argument will be a doozey. You must be careful what you say to Cancer because he has a little magnifying glass to examine any remarks that might hurt his fragile ego. Gemini's remarks can be cutting enough without any magnification.

Cancer, male and female, has a strong attachment to their mother, which is pertinent to Cancer males in relationships. Cancer could find themselves being routinely compared to mother. If you are lucky, it will be just in the realms of cooking and cleaning and baby-making, but in these days of second- and third-generation feminism, mummy could be Condoleezza Rice, with your every move being judged against one of the most powerful women in the world.

On the up side, male Cancers are a real catch because they combine their inherent masculinity and the unusually outward show of feminine energy in their sun sign. Cancer is also a water sign, that is, an emotional sign, with cardinal or outputting active energy. This means that Cancers actively seek out places and people to nurture. They like to woo with their cooking skills and come with more than the average amount of male domestic nous.

Cancer's planet is the moon, and like the moon which controls the tides, they are affected by moodiness. They also avoid confrontation and won't say anything they think will cause an argument, but that does not mean they hide their feelings well. Cancers wear their hearts on their sleeve, so you don't have to be the most perceptive person to know when they are upset with you. Empathetic themselves, they are always the first to laugh or cry with you.

However, Geminis may find these characteristics offputting rather than appealing. Geminis are rarely open to emotional outpourings and like to live life on a much more even keel. Cancer is also looking for someone to nurture and to be nurtured by, which the average Gemini rarely seeks. Ask any mother of a Gemini child. Cuddles are quick and kisses are pecks, as little Gem scrambles from her mother's lap, chattering the whole time, off to explore the world. It is not that Gemini can't love and be loved, just that love is intellectual rather than purely sensual and emotional as the Cancer would have it.

Michael J Fox (Gemini) and Tracey Pollan (Cancer), Nicole Kidman (Gemini) and Tom Cruise (Cancer), and Harrison Ford (Cancer) and Melissa Mathison (Gemini) have all made this one work, at least for a good while. King Edward VIII (Cancer) gave up the throne for his Gemini Wallis Simpson.

Passionate Cancer will fulfil Gemini's physical needs, and cheery Gemini will brighten Cancer's world, but all too soon Gemini's flirting will mortally wound the sensitive Cancer. Be wary.

The Social Cancer
Parties and clubs are not usually Cancer's social style, although they can put on a good bash if they want to.

Dinner parties and intimate pubs are more Cancer's thing, and they are particularly good at making their favourite pub a 'local'. Not for them the industrial clatter of espresso machines and polished concrete. No, they would much prefer the slightly grippy feel of beer-soaked carpet underfoot and the sweet smell of hops and barley fermenting in the ashtrays. Unlike Leo, who goes out of his way to know the name of the barman for sheer kudos value and for the purpose of hauling in favours later, for Cancer, making a homely connection with the person serving the drinks is far more important.

They want their surroundings to be comfortable and they usually prefer their company to fit like a glove as well. Having too many new personalities to deal with at once can unnerve the Crab, so they would prefer to keep new social additions to just one a session. Needless to say, speed dating is not their style.

They are usually great cooks and hospitable hosts who go out of their way to make sure everyone is sated and comfortable. They prefer to overfeed than under, so attend any dinner party armed with an elastic waist as they do not take no for an answer. Their wonderful imagination makes sure that any feast is a visual delight as well.

They are great at organising group outings to the races or on a picnic, and are usually the central point for social life at work. Cancer can be counted on to remember the boss' birthday and pass the hat around for the newborn arrival.

They love a little tipple and are great fun to be with on a big night out. At least, they are for the first half. They tend to hit the wall rather quickly and their impromptu cuddles and whoops of delight can slide into a deep-seated desire to make it home to their own bed or, worse still, beer tears. They are hopeless romantics and can get very 'tired and emotional' if the mood takes them. But that's just it. Cancer is ruled by the moon and its moods, so you may have your Cancer friend pegged as a bit of a wet blanket one night, only to discover the dancing queen within the next.

They are hugely generous and love to ply you with gifts and drinks, and will rarely let you get away with the bill. They are even unhappy with the idea of going dutch. Make sure, however, you never take a Cancer for granted. They make it too easy for you to peg them into a hole and exploit them for all they are worth. They will even seem to enjoy it, but underneath they will be screaming out for you to respect them enough to repay the favour. Cancer will go to any lengths to be loved. That is all they want from life.

How to Woo Your Cancer

Your average Cancer is usually unpretentious in her tastes and can be downright uncomfortable if she thinks she may have to put on any airs and graces, so keep your first date fairly low-key. If you can cook, invite her over to your place and whip up some good tucker, something with strong gutsy tastes and comfort foods, like mash potatoes or dumplings on the side.

Cancers are old-fashioned romantics and will enjoy all the trappings of flowers, chocolates and love poems, and will give you more than your share in return. Make sure your Cancer knows you are enjoying their attentions, because they can become despondent if they think their efforts aren't appreciated.

Cancers can be self-protective, and don't like to leave themselves open to hurt by jumping into bed too soon. Still, they will want you to meet the family quite soon, and if you know what is good for you, you will go along. Don't fear that visiting her parents is barely a step away from walking down the aisle. The Cancer woman simply wants you to meet her family, just as she wants you to meet her friends and her cat – because they are a living, breathing part of her life that she cherishes. If you are going to get to know her, even in the most perfunctory way, you are going to get to know her family.

And whatever you do, be nice and don't make jokes about them when you are back on mutual ground – she won't find them funny.

Gifts for Your Cancer

Cancer's cupboards are usually overflowing with crockery and homewares, but they will gladly accept more, especially large serving platters, because they love feeding the hoards. Cancers can sometimes have a deep-seated feeling that they are being taken advantage of, or that they are overworked or undervalued. If this is your Cancer, a pampering present like perfume or a voucher for a relaxation massage is a thoughtful idea.

A well-chosen card with some thoughtful words is obligatory for a present for your Cancer. Cancers live and breathe by the saying 'it's the thought that counts', and will be put out if those thoughts are not expressed. This can be a bit presumptuous, because they are experts at expressing their own thoughts and don't know how difficult it can be for other people, but a little imagination can go a long way.

LEO/GEMINI

Finally – an ego large enough to laugh in the face of Gemini's flirtations! Leo will not see Gemini's coquetry as an insult to their relationship and as an assault on his ego, but rather as an example of Leo's largesse in sharing his gorgeous and vivacious partner around.

Famous Gemini/Leo matches are wild child Angelina Jolie (Gemini) and her ex, Billy Bob Thornton (Leo), and American royalty John (Gemini) and Jacqueline (Leo) Kennedy (nee Bouvier). Fidel Castro (Leo) and Che Guevara (Gemini) had a revolutionary match in these signs.

An affectionate pair who have a great time together, they will be constantly trying to upstage each other in social settings, but they both love a laugh and can see the funny side of their dramatic coupling. They will be in great demand at dinner parties.

Leos make great mates who are always up for a bit of fun, male and female. It was Leo Edna Ferber who said that 'A woman can look both moral and exciting – if she also looks as if it was quite a struggle.' They are embarrassingly generous, but never turn down a gift, no matter how extravagant, because you will hurt their pride. And they don't take blows to their pride lightly.

They usually possess a belly-trembling chuckle that can break into gales of laughter if really tickled. Their sense of humour is fresh and simple with an eye for the ridiculous. They will take mental notes so that they might appropriate the story for their own use later on. This is where Gemini will provide more than their fair share of intellectual fodder. It won't worry Gemini that Leo is nicking her stories and ideas. There are plenty more where they came from . . .

They have an eye for the decadent and will shell out for the most outrageous things, even if it is rent week. A night out at the pub can be an expensive exercise for the magnanimous Lion.

And all Leo wants in return is your unfettered approval and adoring silence as he tell you another of his usually very funny but sometimes exaggerated stories. Not a bad deal, is it? Gemini thinks – not a bad deal at all . . .

The Social Leo

Leos are most comfortable in the social arena and they know how to play a room to a tee. They are happy to take on the role of entertainer and raconteur if required, keeping spirits up and the conversation interesting. Absurdly generous, they are likely to come back from the bar not only with their round of drinks, but a round of cigars (for smokers and non-smokers alike) and a range of bar snacks. Money is no object when a Leo is entertaining, and their lavish gestures can embarrass some. Don't be embarrassed. Leos show love through indulging their loved-ones with the fruits of their decadence. If you refuse a gift from a Leo, you might find they take it far more personally than you expect.

Leos usually love dancing and show quite a bit of finesse on the dance floor. That is, unless the lubricants have really kicked in, then Leo's larger-than-life dance moves take on an erratic and uncontrolled quality. Limbs that were once thrown about with dramatic flair but always with graceful precision are likely to take on a life of their own. A lurching Leo on the dance floor is a frightening sight indeed. Fortunately, Leo values their self-control above everything, and they rarely lose the plot.

They can be dreadful flirts, but it is only for the thrill of the chase, as they are rarely unfaithful. A single Leo is in their element in a nightclub, as only their large personality can overcome the lights and loud music to shine on through. You will often find your group coming across the odd Leo in a nightclub, engaging you with their witty patter and sparking asides. They are in their element in this situation. There are plenty of new souls to impress and lots of fresh laughs to be had. Sometimes though, they can outstay their welcome, especially if they don't keep their flirtatious nature within reasonable limits, ie, concentrating on one person at a time, and preferably single.

The Leo combination of fixed fire means that they are happy to shine on within themselves. They *are* the main event. They don't need anyone to bounce their light from, although they are always happy to have a straight-man sidekick.

They would rather be out the front than behind the scenes in any situation and love a good opportunity to show off. If they like to sing, they really enjoy a session at a karaoke bar. They are, however, prone to taking themselves a little too seriously and will not take kindly to any jokes or heckles thrown their way, no matter how kindly they are meant. They are good-natured but only up to a point and that point does not include laughing at themselves just because everyone else is. In fact, it is the quickest way to send them into a foul mood.

Leos love the idea of throwing a fantastic party, but they often require the services of someone who is a little more interested in substance over style and has a few clues on how to make things happen. Leo will provide the pizzazz as long as someone else has a handle on the catering. They make attentive hosts who can make a guest feel as if the whole bash has been thrown just for them.

How to Woo Your Leo

If you are planning to woo a Leo, it is prudent to first take out a small loan at a low interest rate. Leos love to pounce quickly and you could find yourself involved in a flurry of theatre and dinner dates snowballing to an early but lavish white wedding.

Make the first date something to remember. Low-key is not in the Leo vocabulary. See a musical, but use whatever influence you have to wrangle backstage passes to meet the actors; go to the tennis, but make sure you watch it from a corporate box. Leos love big dramatic statements and the effort you have gone to will make them feel more special. Don't worry about appearing to be a name-dropper; Leos are the King of the Pride when it comes to big-noting, and they won't bat an eyelid.

Gifts for Your Leo

Leos are extravagant gift givers, so make sure you get in first with a wonderful present. They can't stand cheap and nasty imitations, so always buy the high-quality original, or settle for something else.

Leos love anything that shows them off to their best advantage, so you might consider a voucher for a session of glamour photography. They will love being made up and fussed over, and the resulting photos will take pride of place on their wall. Another idea is to take a favourite photo and have it cropped and blown up and elegantly framed – the bigger the better. Send it with a nice little card telling her to hang it on the wall for her future grand-children, so they will know what a beautiful young woman she was. She will be tickled pink.

A video camera is an expensive idea that is sure to be a big hit. Your Leo will love directing the action from behind the lens as well as hamming it up in front. Make sure you include a tripod, so he can set it up and film his own commentary.

Gold is always appreciated, and rubies and amber are Leo gemstones. Board games with lots of dramatics and interaction, like Pictionary and Charades, are always a lot of fun. (You might want to let him win the first few games, though.)

VIRGO/GEMINI

Both these signs are ruled by the planet Mercury and have a mental approach to life, but where Virgo critiques, Gemini ridicules.

Hugh Grant (Virgo) and Elizabeth Hurley (Gemini) were this combination, as are Courtney Cox (Gemini) and David Arquette (Virgo). Cox and Arquette are great examples of how this Mercury-ruled couple can be so different yet somehow fit. Cox worked her way up the hard way. She was the first woman on TV to say the word 'period' (in a Tampax commercial); she was the cover girl of *People*'s '50 Most Beautiful People' issue, and she's one of the 'Friends'. Arquette is from a Hollywood acting family, he loves wrestling; he's in a rock band; and he looks like your brother's best mate.

But somehow they fell in love. Their honeymoon included stops at a tennis camp, a beach in the Caribbean, and several theme parks where they rode on the roller coasters. Cox shows Virgo how to take life head-on and with energy; Arquette gives Cox his wonderfully Virgo sense of the ridiculous. Virgos have the ability to see the funny side in most things and, although they constantly have an eye for the detail, they relax by being really silly.

Intellectually these two are on a par. They will enjoy good conversations together and they both enjoy mental clarity, but where Gemini likes to race ahead, Virgo likes to bullet point the details, and Gemini can find Virgo's pernickety approach to learning exasperating.

It is the critic in the Virgo that is their inner tormentor. Virgos have an eye for the earthly flaws. They automatically notice the imperfection in everything. Gemini doesn't usually take criticism too personally but she might ark up if it is constant. And with Virgo, it can be constant. This may be a difficult point, but Gemini should know that the Virgo critiques everything, including themselves.

Caring and serving others is what Virgos do best. Virgo is the caregiver. He will attend to Gemini's needs, but Gemini should try to be aware of his intense desire for sacred space. Virgos are the loners of the zodiac and every sock of yours that they pick up is a reminder of how nice a place of their own would be. Gemini would do well to give Virgo a space that she doesn't enter, so he can pick every speck of lint off the floor if he wants.

The Social Virgo

At a party, Virgo can come across as impenetrable, a cool cavernous fortress with a moat as deep and as wide as the one Scorpio built for himself. Self-assured and steady as a rock, they can sometimes intimidate others with their dry wit and crackling intelligence. A cool piercing Virgo stare will make the most well-rehearsed pick-up line stick in the throat of the deliverer. Virgos are not into frippery. They are even less tolerant of the crude or rude, so if you are going to tackle one with a pick-up line, make sure it is vaguely tasteful.

Some find the assured Virgo posture irresistibly sexy; others find it daunting. Don't be overawed. The too-cool-for-school image is merely a defence. Underneath the elegant posturing, Virgos are warm, funny and not a little bit silly. They enjoy a clever sense of humour and are quick with the one-liners. You might get the impression that Virgo is a bit of a snob, but nothing could be further from the truth. They are not social climbers at all and they would rather die than wear a flashy label. The Virgo is much happier occupying the middle rung of society and she would be mortified to be thought of as a pompous high-flier.

Most of the time, their cool exterior is masking a certain shyness that is fairly easily overcome. Their acute sense of timing and tempered sense of style means they are smoothies on the dance floor, but although it might not be obvious, they are usually waiting anxiously for you to take the lead. Virgos are most at home around a dinner party table where their intelligence and wit can shine through. They are great storytellers and full of interesting information about a wide range of topics that they convey in an easy manner. Their sense of humour can tend towards the self-deprecating and they rarely turn their keen wit on others, although when they do, watch out!

Virgos are purists in every sense and they will approach their tipple in the same way. They will either be staunchly brand loyal or have a particular way that their drink has to be served. The fictional character James Bond had some Virgo tendencies, including his penchant for his martinis to be shaken (not stirred). You will meet Virgos who eschew drinking altogether in preference for keeping their body pure.

Virgos are fantastic at throwing parties. After all, their motto is 'I serve' and they fit comfortably into the role of making sure everything is humming, that drinks are constantly topped up and the conversation is rattling along at one hundred miles an hour. If anything, they could ask for a little more help, as they are usually unwilling to hand over the reins of any project big or small, even passing around a bowl of chips. Virgos are notorious perfectionists and it is not that they don't trust you to do a good job, it's just that they don't trust you to do a good job!

How to Woo Your Virgo

Virgos will be drawn out by warmth and enjoy a thoughtful compliment, but will be repelled by overt shows of physical affection or gushiness.

Keep your first date simple. See a film or a show with coffee afterwards, because Virgos can be a little shy but are never lost for words when given something to critique. If the spark is there, you could find yourself talking till dawn, ranging over current affairs, music, politics, religion and the meaning of life.

Don't assume that because your Virgo is the embodiment of stylish understatement that you will be expected to be the same. Virgos are often quite attracted to the outlandish or the quirky. Above all, they treasure scrupulous honesty, so be yourself and no one else.

Gifts for Your Virgo

Virgos have green fingers, so presents such as gardening tools could be a good idea, or a bonsai might put them on the path to a healthy hobby – bonsais require a lot of care and attention and a judicious pruning every now and then, skills that Virgos excel in.

Their colour preferences are all shades of blue, dark brown and beige. If you are looking for clothes, be sure to err on the generous size rather than mistakenly get them something too tight-fitting. Virgos don't like revealing any more flesh than is prudent.

They usually like reading nonfiction, so biographies and reference books are good ideas. A magazine subscription is a gift in the same vein. A good filofax or digital notebook is sure to be put to rigorous use. Lavender soap, bath salts or perfume will soothe that Virgo worried mind.

Virgos are meticulous people and appreciate it if you pay attention to the detail, so make sure the gift is perfectly wrapped, and the card is signed with something personal and fitting.

LIBRA/GEMINI

Love is in the air! Both these signs are affectionate, fun loving, like a social life, and love to entertain and travel.

Gemini Paul McCartney had two great Libra partnerships – Linda Eastman and John Lennon. Both relationships were characterised by how they related on an intellectual level; in Lennon he found a musical muse, and in Linda a political and spiritual peer. Writer Arthur Miller (Libra) and Marilyn Monroe (Gemini) were another example of this pairing.

Generally, Librans are beautiful people with a sense of style and serenity about them. Just about any advertisement about air freshener tries to portray the Libran ideal – beautiful light-filled house, tasteful throw pillows, gorgeous children and sexy Mum, classical music playing in the background. Librans look like they have it all, and that is how they want it to be.

But sometimes life isn't smooth, and they can look very ruffled in bad weather. If something is weighing down an aspect of Libra's life, they will be pulling hard on the other end of the scales trying to balance this discrepancy.

The Libran symbol of the scales can be misleading. You could be forgiven for thinking of Libra as perfectly even-handed and even-tempered. This will probably be your initial impression, but he is much more of a meddler than that! Scales are not perfectly weighted each side all of the time, and when they aren't they are in a state of flux. Libra will always try and pull the scales back. If you have an opinion about something, Libra will look at you kindly and tell you in perfectly even tones why you are perfectly wrong.

And then he will tell you in the same even tones why you are, in fact, perfectly correct.

In this way they can appear to be very similar to Gemini, who are renowned for moving the goal posts in any argument, but that is because they don't see any real need for a fixed position. They just enjoy the argument for its own sake. This is a different motivation to Libra, who wants people to see that there are at least two sides to every story. They see it more as a social service, where Gemini just does it for fun.

Sexually, neither is jealous or demanding, and when Gemini wants to experiment, Libra goes along for the ride. They will go through wads of money, but otherwise are a perfect match.

The Social Libra

Librans make an art form out of being social. Many of their life's goals revolve around meeting and greeting and making the perfect union, and they take this attitude out into the world with them, especially into a party situation. You would think this would make them the perfect hosts. But in fact, a Libran party can be quite a stressful situation for all involved. Like a little kid planning their first ever five-year-old party, Libra can often have far too many of the details already worked out in their mind – who's going to talk to whom, what the weather will be like, the ambience, the music, the food. They can picture it so clearly, they are in danger of being sorely disappointed when things inevitably don't go exactly to plan.

The more important the gathering, the more Libra will fret. A Libran woman planning her wedding is the classic nubile nightmare. Just the seating for the table arrangements will take more than a few weeks. Libra's innate sense of style and grace will mean the selection of the dress and the flowers will come naturally, but beyond that, the Libran woman will drive herself crazy trying to organise the most perfect night of her life. After all, this is when her Libran ideals come together at once – marriage and partnership, friends and family, and beautiful things in a gorgeous setting.

You can allow Libra that on her once-in-a-lifetime special day. But just once, it would be nice if Libra could throw a small relaxed dinner party without all the expectation placed upon it. You might think that that is exactly what you agreed to considering the flippant way Libra dished out the invitation. Just a casual affair, a few friends, come as you are. So you turn up in your comfy gear, bottle of cheapish plonk in hand, ready for a chilled-out evening with close friends.

Don't get too comfortable though, because you will soon be introduced to Libra's friend, complete with meaningful glances and an introduction befitting a speech inducting you into the Hall of Fame. Libra is a shameless matchmaker and can't resist an opportunity to hook people up. There is no such thing as happily single in Libra's world. That surely has to be an oxymoron. For

Libra, relationships are the key to happiness of any kind, and seeing as they're so intent on making sure everyone is happy, the least they can do is make sure you have opportunities to get hitched. It is an act of love on their behalf, so accept gracefully and try to make the most of the opportunity to meet someone new.

They are not huge on self-control and can get a little tiddly if left unchecked. Some Librans have been known to calm their pre-party nerves with a few heart-starters only to find themselves a little too refreshed to see the event to its natural conclusion. Some are even lucky to be able to usher the first few guests in, so if you are throwing a party with a Libra, suggest other ways to de-stress if you see your Libra getting wound up about the canapés. Deep breathing, a long shower or even a last-minute trip to the supermarket will make sure Libra is on track for a great evening and short-circuit them from hitting the drinks trolley too early.

How to Woo Your Libra

If you happen to fall under the spell of Libra, don't surrender too quickly. Let them flirt with you for a while. Even if they push towards a relationship, imagine that it's just the scales tipping to compensate for your cooler attitude. Libra has so much fun pursuing relationships that they will love you for dragging out the anticipation.

First dates should be fairly conservative and tasteful. When choosing a restaurant, don't go for anything remotely tacky. When she says dinner and a show, she means that nice little Italian place and *Les Miserables*, not a theme restaurant with an all-you-can-eat buffet.

Don't go anywhere too modern, with concrete floors and clattering coffee machines. Libra is very sensitive to the beauty of her surroundings, and will be much more relaxed with dim lighting and gentle music.

Gifts for Your Libra

Whatever you buy a Libran, make sure you give them the receipt as well so they can take it back. It's not that they don't appreciate your gift, it is just that they have their own sense of style that is hard to pick. Even they find it hard to choose. So she will go back to the store with the pepper grinder you gave her, receipt in hand, spend fifteen minutes looking through all the other pepper grinders, weighing up their pros and cons, and end up leaving the shop with the one you bought in the first place. But she will be satisfied that the right decision has been made.

Libran colours are green and blue. For gardening Librans (they love to be out in the green beauty), a coffee-table gardening book would be appreciated. Self-indulgent luxuries go down well, and a carefully chosen antique will be accepted with great joy.

SCORPIO/GEMINI

Gemini will light Scorpio's embers, but they will soon find out that sex isn't everything. Scorpio is inflexible to Gemini's fickle nature, and Gemini will be under the constant scrutiny of Scorpio's suspicion. In turn, Scorpio is setting himself up for heartbreak by falling for Gemini's light-hearted approach to love.

This is a matching for the upwardly mobile, especially enigmatic Scorpio women marrying well. Prince Rainier (Gemini) and Grace Kelly (Scorpio) had a fairytale romance with this match. Johnny Depp (Gemini) famously tattooed the name of one his exes, Scorpio Winona Ryder, onto his arm. Albert Camus (Scorpio) and Jean Paul Sartre (Gemini) shared an intellectual match with these signs.

Scorpios require solid security within a relationship, without feeling that they have a doormat as a mate. This is a precarious balance and will be learned by both partners over time.

Gemini is intelligent enough to learn this game and will enjoy playing it for a little while – until she realises how high the stakes are. Geminis love to play games but only if they are for fun. Scorpio's games are never just for fun.

If Gemini can convince Scorpio to lighten up a little and Scorpio can convince Gemini to consider his feelings, these problems should be resolvable. The longer a relationship lasts with a Scorpio, the more secure it tends to become. They are naturally suspicious and need a lot of reassurance, so Gemini will have to learn to placate as a matter of habit.

If the relationship does end, Gemini should be warned that they are unlikely to skip away scot-free as they have done before. There will be hints of this early on. Scorpios carry the deceits of the past with a hurt as fresh as if it was yesterday. Many an ill-mannered Scorpio has bored a first date to tears with vitriolic stories of his ex. This can turn into full-blown self-pity, which is not attractive to anyone, and poor old Scorpio can become his own worst enemy. A Scorpio is better young and fresh. A Scorpio with baggage is hard to convince.

Yet Scorpios possess bucketloads of passion. You will not find a more passionate sign in the zodiac. Once convinced of the other's commitment and deeply in love, Scorpio will lavish Gemini with flattery and affection. The heart of Scorpio is a delicious pool to drown in.

There *are* problems, though. At the heart of it, Gemini loves people and Scorpio likes privacy. Be careful with one another.

The Social Scorpio

Scorpios are generally more your one-on-one type of person. They are happy to go with you to any party and enjoy the refreshments and the entertainment, but they usually want to stick close. At dinner parties, they generally resist group conversation, preferring instead to turn to the person next to them and engage their interest.

Socially, Scorpios like to have a foil for their own personality. A Taurus is perfect for this purpose as they are a diametrically opposite in character because they sit exactly opposite each other on the zodiac wheel. Scorpio's cool intellect is balanced by Taurus' warm conversation; Scorpio's vampish sexuality is juxtaposed with Taurus' homely appearance and so on.

Scorpios are well aware of the intrigue that surrounds them when they play the mysterious lone wolf, but it can be a little lonely if they don't have a trusty friend to help forge the real connections. That is where the foil comes in. Scorpio can continue to appear cool and mysterious, while her erstwhile friend makes sure the invites keep coming and the diary is full.

Super competitive, they will make a game out of any social situation to keep themselves amused. For some, it is snaring the most eligible bachelor in the room, for others it is a bit more risky and involves consuming large amounts of inebriating substances. Drinking games take on a deadly intensity with any Scorpio and should not be entered into by the faint-hearted, although Scorpio is more likely going to be the one to overdo it.

This will happen at least once for every Scorpio. And they usually only do it once because, having discovered their limit, they hate losing control and feel embarrassment with burning intensity. In fact, they are sometimes in danger of reducing their life's experience down to the things that they are pretty sure they have a handle on, so there is no opportunity for getting red in the face.

There is the lone wolf Scorpio, but there is also the zealot groupie Scorpio who throws himself into one cause or another. This is the sign of sex and religion don't forget, so Scorpios are just as likely to get themselves deeply involved in some sort of club-life, whether that be karate, scouting, political activism or the Church of the Latter-Day Motorcycle Rebels. Whatever it is, they will be true converts, running the cake stall and cornering people on the bus, letting them know how much it has changed their life.

And this is true. Scorpio is all about change, the transition from death to life, so Scorpios spend their lives looking for deeper meaning in their existence, evolving this process through many stages, and this includes their social interactions. Scorpio is looking for rebirth in every relationship, no matter how fleeting it may seem.

How to Woo Your Scorpio

If you go to a party together, you need to master the art of letting your Scorpio go and reeling him in. Scorpios generally feel a bit on edge in a social situation with a partner, as they can see too much danger in flirtatious situations and they are very quick to jealousy.

Make sure you have a proprietary hand on the small of their back when you are introducing them to people. Meet their eyes across the room, and if you see they need a drink, get them one.

Break away from the group to go up behind them and whisper in their ear that they look fantastic. You will have the hairs on the back of their neck standing up in excitement.

Gifts for Your Scorpio

Scorpios are intense and passionate, with a love of mystery and secrets. They get as much pleasure wondering what's inside the box as they do opening it.

They love to investigate – think about mysteriously giving them only a clue to the present. For instance, if you are planning on surprising them with a romantic weekend for their birthday (for these sex addicts, this idea will fill them with joy), wrap up a carry-on luggage bag, packed with nothing but black lacy lingerie. Their eyes will sparkle with delight as they put two and two together. It's at that moment you can take the plane tickets out of your top pocket.

Giving the gift in secret will titillate them even more. If you have bought a bracelet for her, wait until you are at a party. Pull her away mysteriously during the evening to somewhere secluded to give her your gift. After a passionate embrace, make a show of going back into the party as if nothing has happened.

Some Scorpios like to flirt with the occult, so they might like a crystal ball, Tarot cards, Rune stones or a book on white magic. Scorpios also love water and they like to swim, so a new swimsuit might be a good idea. Exotic perfumes, satin sheets or something a little kinky will tease their sensual tastes.

SAGITTARIUS/GEMINI

It won't last long, but oh what a wild ride it will be! Gemini and Sagittarius sit exactly opposite in the zodiac and are fascinated by each other. They especially enjoy picking over each other's brains, for both have many and varied interests. They will talk for hours, plan excursions and get along like an oxygen-fed house on fire.

Opposites of the zodiac often make successful couples, even though at first glance they may not seem to have much in common. In fact, all opposites come from compatible elemental groups (fire/air or earth/water) and all are of the same quadruplicity (cardinal, fixed or mutable), so they are more compatible than someone of the sign before or after the opposite.

There have been some interesting father/son combinations in this pairing. Sagittarius singer Jakob Dylan has a lot to live up to in his Gemini father, Bob Dylan. The same could have been said for John F Kennedy Jnr (Sagittarius) and his father, John F Kennedy (Gemini).

Sagittarians are explorers both of the world and of the mind. They love to travel and experience new people, places and cultures, but they are also happy to sit at home in front of an open fire, glass of red by the hearth, exploring ideas and thoughts with good friends. They generally love to find out about people and explore philosophy with strangers. Sagittarians have been known to take several hours buying a litre of milk after starting up a conversation on the bus or at the local shops.

Sagittarians can inadvertently stray, especially if the affair is with someone unusual or famous and thus is an experience that will never be repeated. The cliche about having to always try things once was no doubt made up by a Sagittarian, and this is inclusive of sexual conquests in both males and females.

Geminis understand this and are equally in danger of

straying, for similar reasons. Sagittarius will probably find it harder to forgive than Gemini, though, and if this hypocrisy is too apparent, there will be arguments. The reason that Gemini can forgive and forget more easily is that, as an air sign, she is able to intellectualise emotional issues more easily, whereas fire signs (Sag) take an intuitive approach, so their emotions are mixed in with intellect and perceptions.

This fire may burn out when it gets really serious and moves into the bedroom. Unfortunately, neither of this pair is particularly demonstrative and neither likes to take too much responsibility for keeping the relationship afloat. If it does end (and you really don't know what a good thing you are onto until it is gone), it will end amicably, and you will probably remain good mates.

The Social Sagittarius

Like Leo, no party is ever big enough for two Sagittarians. If two Sags ever come across each other in a party environment, there is sure to be a showdown, twenty paces at dawn. Only one will survive. At first, the two will circle each other (metaphorically, of course). Sag One tosses in a one-liner. Sag Two recognises an opponent. He smirks, and counters with small joke. Sag One will bide her time, waiting for an opportunity to tell one of her hilarious tales, usually set in a far-off country. Sag Two will brush off this attack with a marvellous rejoinder, something truly pants-wetting, that just happens to be in a country even more remote than the setting for Sag One's vignette. And so on.

Eventually, after at first entertaining, tiring, bewildering and then alienating everyone else in the group with their horsey posturing, everyone will wander off, leaving the Sags locked in a centaur to centaur tussle for supremacy, hysterically countering each other's tall tales with even taller ones. Each Sag needs to prove that they are more funny, more worldly, more spiritual and more well read than the other, completely forgetting that their true aim was to entertain, something that they are both now failing dismally at.

Sad but true. And at least most Sags will admit it, especially after a few lubricating beverages. Whoever made up the saying 'in vino veritas' had just been on the town with a Sagittarian. Sags are happy to spill their guts on most things when stone cold sober. When they have had a few, they are happy to spill everyone else's as well. They have many reasons for doing this and only one of them commendable. They value the truth above everything, and they would never let a secret out that they wouldn't be quite happy to have revealed about themselves. But as I have just pointed out, there are very few things that a Sag will keep hidden in their own closet, so their temperature reading for other people's secrets is usually a good ten degrees cooler than most other people's assessments. The key is, make sure your Sag knows when you are letting them in on a Big One. It won't guarantee that the story will never be told, but at least Sag will have the good grace to feel guilty when they finally do spill it.

Sags don't do anything by halves, so if they are out for a big night on the town, plan for a big morning as well. Their physical stamina is legendary and their enthusiasm unbounded – a lethal combination for most other humanoids. They like to keep the party moving, both conversationally and energy-wise, but they also like to keep everyone moving physically, and they are usually the ones pushing to move on to a nightclub, just when everyone was settling in nicely.

They can be wildly generous or happy to bot freely, especially as they have usually just lost their wallet/car/shirt in some strange-but-true situation that they are bound to bounce back out of, usually with more change in their pocket than before the drama ensued. Their 'easy come, easy go' attitude has been reinforced by years of them falling straight back onto their feet after the most unlikely disasters, so you won't mind if you help them out of this last scrape, will you? You know they're good for it!

How to Woo Your Sagittarius

Intrigue them, surprise them, tantalise them, worry them, just don't ever bore them. You could take Sagittarius just about anywhere for your first date as long as it is just the tiniest bit exotic. McDonald's and a blockbuster movie are not going to do the trick. But a Ninja film and duck soup on formica tables in a café in Chinatown will charm her. If it is a new experience, she will love it whether or not she liked the movie, and she will love debating the merits of Ninja films with you late into the night.

Later on, take her away as often as you can afford it. It doesn't have to be an overnight trip, but springing a surprise flight to the capital city for dinner and a show and a night on the town will delight her. A trip to the coast to fossick about in antique stores or an afternoon at the wineries in the hills will have her glowing. Check out river cruises that might take you to the nearest port for a seafood dinner – such exotic pleasures can be surprisingly affordable.

Gifts for Your Sagittarius

Sagittarians love to give presents as an expression of their warm personality. They usually agonise for weeks over what to buy, and almost always spend an embarrassing amount of money – money is not that important to the Sagittarius, and after all, what price a friend or loved one? Jupiter is the giver of wealth and is associated with prosperity, laughter and happiness, so it's not surprising that Sagittarians are at their best when gifts are being exchanged, such as at Christmas.

Sadly, these gifts are not always on the mark, but they would be mortified if they thought they had got it wrong, so be gentle.

When buying for your Sagittarius, remember they usually feel comforted by their colours indigo and royal purple. Displays of honesty are very important to them, so it really is the thought that counts. If the giver forgets to write a card, then the gift is as good as flawed.

Books always go down well, especially if you have read it so they can discuss it with you later. Clothes are often a nice idea, as they usually can't stand shopping for themselves, and have a very laissez-faire sense of style that will accommodate most things.

Anything that will give them a new experience is accepted with joy: a shiatsu massage (massages are good for Sagittarius as they are generally not physically demonstrative); a hot-air balloon ride; a night out at a cocktail bar trying everything on the menu (they can hold their drink); tickets to a show; or enrolment in a course of life drawing/salsa dancing/theology classes.

CAPRICORN/GEMINI

Capricorn needs the security of walls and floors, while metaphorically Gemini likes to sleep in the open air; Capricorn needs routine and a regular pay cheque to feel at ease, Gemini feels queasy whenever you mention either of these things; Capricorn worries about security, while Gemini worries about keeping her freedom.

All is not lost, though – with understanding, Capricorn can show Gemini how to ground her constant curiosity, and Gemini can show Capricorn how domination only destroys relationships and help him to develop his sensual potential.

It can also work if the Gemini is much older than the Capricorn. Gemini is one of the youngest signs; their natives often look remarkably young for their age and they have the energy of a teenager into their twilight years. Conversely, Capricorns seem to grow young, rather than grow old. They are born thirty, and spend their youth and early twenties growing their body into its rightful age.

After the death of his Libran wife, Linda, Paul McCartney (Gemini) married the much younger Heather Mills, whose Capricorn sun sign probably makes her a more compatible age match. Kylie Minogue (Gemini) and her French lover, Olivier Martinez (Capricorn), followed in the path of Johnny Depp (Gemini) and his French wife, Vanessa

Paradis (Capricorn). Elvis Presley (Capricorn) and Priscilla Presley (Gemini) were also this pairing.

Most would love to have skipped all those tiresome early years, having to be friends with immature brats and having no control over their destiny. The teenage years are especially painful for a Capricorn. Teenage rebellion holds no sway with him; he just wants to get out of school, so he can start earning a wage and take some control of his life.

Gemini wanted to skip school, too, but for completely different reasons. These are two people whose life philosophies are completely at odds, but that does not mean there is no hope. There will be moments when Capricorn will mutter, 'But what do you stand for, which side of the fence are you on?' while at the same time that Gemini thinks, 'oh, not everything is so cut and dried . . .'

But equally there will be moments of complete joy, when Gemini will convince Cappy to skinny dip just this once, or when Capricorn will indulge Gem in the comfort of an absolute.

The Social Capricorn

Capricorns can't resist using a party or gathering as a business networking opportunity. At least that is how it can come across, before Cap has even had a chance to let his hair down. Poor old Cappie, most things he does are interpreted as something to do with his practical, steadfast, money-hungry and status-thirsty Capricorn side, but it is not always the case. Sometimes Cap can just come across as a little too pressing and a little too forward because he doesn't quite know how to give himself over to the conversation. Is it a crime to ask too many questions? And is it any wonder that he doesn't think his life or his thoughts are remotely conversation worthy? Capricorns are always being told they are terminally boring. Not really a boost to the old self-esteem when you are trying to chat up a pretty lady, is it?

But after Cap has warmed up, and after he has stopped quizzing you on your expected gross output for the financial year to date, he might even reveal a few of his funnier observations on the party at hand. The Cap sense of humour is wry and dry and just a little bit wicked, especially when it comes to summing up a character or a situation in a few funny words. For this reason, they are mostly observers rather than initiators or participators. They will get involved but usually only if they are in total control. They are either standing on the sidelines or running the show. There is no in-between.

And they are fabulous at running the show. Every need will be met, every whim catered for with ruthless efficiency. A Capricorn party is a seamless affair, if a little lacking in imagination. But the drinks are cold, the food is hot, the entertainment starts on time and the speeches are short and sweet – what more could you ask for?

They are loyal and honest friends who enjoy a 'less is more' approach to gathering and keeping friends. They are ambitious in many areas of their life, but they are not usually the type to go and count up their Christmas cards as a booster for their self-esteem. It must have been a Capricorn who said you should only be able to fit your good friends on one hand, otherwise you are spreading yourself too thin.

There is, of course, the other type of Capricorn, the hip as hip rock star Cap whose commanding presence makes everyone else in the room check their cool credentials nervously. Don't forget, David Bowie, Patti Smith, Michael Stipe, Annie Lennox and Janis Joplin are all Capricorns. When you think Capricorn, you also think independent, powerful, seriously charismatic, and never too eager to please. These guys demand an entourage of adoring fans just for waking up in the morning. If your Capricorn friend happens to be more rock star than rookie, you have got yourself a goldmine of invites and open doors. These Caps are usually way too cool to truly take advantage of freebies, so you can make yourself a nice little social life using up Cap's unused drink cards or passes to this and that.

How to Woo Your Capricorn

Dress well, for goodness sake, and check that your nails are clean. Capricorn does not demand a great beauty, but he does look for taste and grooming. If you are arranging the restaurant, choose somewhere with an established reputation, and an even better wine list. Capricorn won't quibble about the prices but he knows good service, so you don't want to risk a new restaurant.

He will love talking about his work and family, but you may wonder after a while if he wants to know anything about you. Of course he does, he just doesn't want to be impertinent about how he asks. Sometimes Capricorn is so uptight about manners that he can seem quite rude. Gently introduce yourself into the conversation and you will see his interest pick up. Be sure to put in a few points about your breeding, for example that your grandfather fought in World War II. Leave out that your Dad dodged the draft by engaging in the longest-running arts degree ever recorded by a university, at least for now.

Take mental notes on the hobbies of his mother and sisters. Down the track you can please him no end by taking his mother out for shopping and coffee. He probably still lives with her, so you are going to get to know her pretty well anyway.

Gifts for Your Capricorn

Practical, sturdy, lasts forever. Go all-out on the quality of a gift, but don't buy brand names unless you want to hear snorts of derision.

Capricorns like homewares and tools, but they also like to be treated as though they have interests other than the practical. It may seem strange, but Capricorn will not hesitate to buy herself whatever she needs, even though she will never buy those things that she might whimsically wish for. Capricorn does not put a high enough price on her own happiness, so it is up to her friends and loved ones to litter her life with frivolity.

Capricorns love a gift that has taken a lot of time and

patience to make. Their colour preferences are indigo, dark brown and black. But the key word, whatever you buy, is quality.

AQUARIUS/GEMINI

Aquarius understands Gemini's inconsistency and will not take it to heart. In fact, Aquarius is likely to be just as inconsistent himself!

Aquarius, like Gemini, can't stand commitment and will do anything to get out of confirming a date or committing to a time. If you invite an Aquarian friend out to dinner on Friday night, no matter how far in advance you ask, don't expect an answer until Friday morning. Don't ever ask for a time. Even if they volunteer one, it will bear no relation to the actual time that they arrive.

For this reason, it may take some time before these two get it together, if at all. Neither prioritises relationships and both are likely to let opportunities slide, and then be surprised when the other doesn't call. Gemini is probably the one who will make the first move, but Aquarius had better follow up if he is interested, as Gemini is more flighty than even himself.

Aquarians are radicals; they like to think outside the square, and the box it came in as well. Geminis are attracted to new ideas and new concepts, so they will find this very attractive. Hollywood's first outwardly gay couple Ellen DeGeneres (Aquarius) and Anne Heche (Gemini) were a great example of this. Australian bards Henry Lawson (Gemini) and Banjo Patterson (Aquarius) were also this pairing.

Any Aquarian will tell you that *Who's Who* is littered with Aquarians, and it is true that they do seem to have more than their fair share of high achievers, especially in the sciences, filmmaking and writing. They also have a good sprinkling of strong women and famous feminists – Alice Walker, Colette, Virginia Woolf, Betty Friedan, Susan B Anthony and Germaine Greer all have Aquarian sun signs.

These two share a taste for the bizarre and meeting new people, and Aquarius can't get enough of Gemini's cheery attitude. Aquarians love the idea of people, but as long as it is only people in the abstract. This is fine with Gemini, who also prefers ideas over sensuality. This means that the sex runs hot and cold, but that is how both these signs like it. Neither needs constant physical attention; in fact, they prefer friendship and flirtation over sweaty copulation most of the time. In marriage, these two are affectionate companions more than passionate lovers, but they are much more likely to make it to their golden anniversary hand in hand than some of their more tempestuous peers.

Gemini is the seeker of knowledge, while Aquarius claims to have the knowledge. An intellectual match.

The Social Aquarius

Socially, Aquarians are more likely to be keeping the wheels turning at any gathering than being a mere mingling cog. They are the sign of universal gatherings, so they are often the organisers rather than the life of the party.

This suits their keenly observant personality down to the ground. They would much rather have the odd bemusing conversation with the flotsam to judge the temperature of a party, than be forced to be the star of the group. That doesn't mean they are not capable of 'holding court'. In fact, when they deign to dazzle you with their brilliance, you can be sure their light will outshine even the most riotous Leo – but they would usually prefer if you did the talking. You reveal more of yourself that way.

You can pick any Aquarius on the dance floor by their unusual dress and their decidedly different moves. Not for them the 'step-together, step-together' with a 'white-man's overbite'. No, if Aquarius is going to shake their booty, you can be sure they will be moving to a different drum than the rest of the crowd. They are usually well aware of the sort of impression they are giving to others, so they won't embarrass themselves with any unsavoury dance techniques, but they will get themselves noticed.

If your Aquarian friend decides to really break out and indulge in a few beverages, the quiet and thoughtful veneer is soon shed. Don't forget that the Aquarian motto is 'I know'. They can go from delicately teasing out everyone's opinions one minute to boorishly dominating conversation with their own political beliefs the next.

But usually they are a paragon of moderacy. Besides, they enjoy psychoanalysis too much to give that up!

They are not loyal to any one place, and are unlikely to have a local drinking haunt. Rather, they like to go where things are happening, so they are usually up on the latest clubs and bars around town, although preferably away from the mainstream. They generally enjoy music or theatre or both, so they can be a bit of a walking, talking gig guide, but be prepared for anything if you take them up on one of their suggestions. The Aquarian idea of a nice night at the theatre is more likely to contain interpretative dance and full-frontal nudity than your run-of-the-mill production of *The King and I*.

In a party situation, Aquarians are natural flirts but in a combative way. Flattery is not usually a tool of choice, in fact, most Aquarians feel more comfortable when they have riled up the object of their affections and they are engaged in an intellectual tussle. This unusual strategy can have surprisingly good results and can also get Aquarius over the next hurdle – the physical. Aquarius is not a very touchy-feely sign and they are much more comfortable putting you in a playful headlock than a romantic clinch, at least for now. In summary, being wooed by an Aquarian can feel a little like being teased by your best friend's older brother.

How to Woo Your Aquarius

Approach from the side, never head on, as there is nothing that will scare an Aquarian off more than a full-frontal romance attack. They can't stand romantic nonsense like roses and candlelight, which they see as so predictable, tacky and unimaginative.

At this point, rose wilting pathetically, you may just want to put down your heart-shaped box of chocolates and run. No one would blame you. Not even Aquarius would blame you, and they will probably be quite remorseful next time they see you, once they've had a chance to calm down.

It is not that Aquarius really thinks you have no imagination (although she does love things to be a little bit unusual), she just got a bit of a shock. You were thinking of a nice night out, all she saw was a marriage proposal and a mortgage and a dozen snotty-nosed kids. The bars clanged down around her. She felt short of breath, claustrophobic, so she shot out the worst insult in her repertoire – that you are ordinary.

Now, what you have to do is very simple. Be her friend. But not just any old friend, make sure you are the wittiest and most intelligent friend on the planet, with a hint of mystery about you. Engage, intrigue, woo her all at the same time. Walk away. Let some time pass, hold out for several weeks if you can. Then 'bump' into her; make an impression, make lots of eye contact and then make an excuse. Get out of there. Then the next day, send her a little gift, something really unusual, with no subtext of romance.

You must have her thinking that she is the one doing the wooing and that you are the one playing hard to get. This goes double-plus if the Aquarian is male. Whatever you do, attack from left of field – they can fall in love, and they make wonderful, stable, faithful partners who are never short on conversation once in love; you just have to convince them it is their idea.

Aquarians are also not adverse to email. This is another way of casually engaging their attention and showing off your witty repartee.

Gifts for Your Aquarius
Aquarians generally like unusual or quirky gifts. But quirky should not be read as 'whacky'. And Aquarians hate anything that is crude or rude.

For something unusual, head to any antiques shop or second-hand bookshop and it will be full of stuff for your Aquarian. Ancient Tibetan mountain bells, a shoe snob, a collection of *Boy's Annuals* from the 1950s, a barber's clock that tells the time in mirror image – you get the idea. If it makes you stop and muse, 'isn't that unusual?', you are probably on the right track.

The Aquarian's colour is aqua. They may not wear it, but they seem to have it around, even more so than other signs and their colours, often in their bedroom colour schemes.

Some Aquarians like techno gadgets, the newer the better. A wrist-watch mobile telephone will elicit a squeal of delight. Others are on a more humanitarian and environmental bent, and will like anything you buy from Greenpeace, Oxfam or Community Aid Abroad. Don't forget your Aquarian when travelling. That is the perfect time to stock up on one-of-a-kinds.

PISCES/GEMINI

Gemini is likely to be very attracted to the Piscean dreamy nature, but his thoughtlessness will too easily hurt the emotional Pisces and his mischievousness will bruise her sensitive spirit. Eventually, Gemini will be frustrated by Pisces' reluctance to deal with reality, and overwhelmed by the Piscean need to be adored.

This can be a very poetic coupling. Gemini has the requirements to communicate the Pisces dreamings. Beat writers and friends Allen Ginsberg (Gemini) and Jack Kerouac (Pisces) had this relationship; Kerouac held the intangible fleetingly and through his conversations with Ginsberg, and shaped it into a tangible form in their poetry and novels. Funnymen Dean Martin (Gemini) and Jerry Lewis (Pisces), and high-fliers Donald Trump (Gemini) and Ivana Trump (Pisces) were this pairing, as are tennis couple Lleyton Hewitt (Pisces) and Kim Clijsters (Gemini).

Gemini will have to take the reins a little, whether male or female. Piscean women like to be romanced and taken care of. She might put up a protest but only because she thinks you may be a modern man who would like to hear it.

It is the same for the Pisces male. Let a Pisces man open doors and buy you dinner and generally think he is the tough one. He needs to wear the mask society taught him to wear as a little boy – because boys don't cry. But before long, he will be writing you poetry, getting clucky over pictures of baby animals and bawling his eyes out with you when you're sad.

Keep the first date fairly formal. She loves to dress up and will be disappointed if she can't really wow you with her make-up and her clothes. The less relaxed the better; Pisces prefer to wear the masks of formality.

Elizabeth Taylor is a famous Pisces who must have had a Gemini somewhere in her legions of lovers. Pisces often have striking eyes and Taylor was no exception. With her beautiful violet eyes, her glorious cleavage, and her penchant for bourbon and failed love affairs, she is Pisces personified. No wonder Gemini is smitten.

But there are problems, for the most part about who is going to wear the pants in the relationship. With both Pisces and Gemini it almost always has to be the other person. Neither sign likes to take the reins. Pisces can be very indecisive, and seem to mutate with the whims of others rather than make a firm decision. Gemini usually lets others make the decisions because she can see the benefits and detriments of both sides and doesn't particularly want the responsibility of the decision. So you can see we have a problem when it comes to paying the electricity bill.

But neither will be too fussed if the lights turn off around them; there will be other problems on their mind. Pisces needs someone to love them, Gemini needs someone to have fun with. Pisces veers with their emotions, whereas Gemini very rarely lets emotions become a part of the equation.

Both possess qualities that the other could well do with, and persistence will pay off, but they must be prepared for a long road ahead. Compromise is the key word.

The Social Pisces

Pisces are either on or off. There is no denying that. Some days they have all the energy in the world to give to a social situation. Other days, not even Dr Phil could get a coherent response from them. They only have so much energy to give, and once it is used up, it is like trying to start a car with a flat battery. You just can't.

So don't take it personally if your Pisces friend is a little, well, mute at your next party. Yours is probably the last in a line of a few social engagements and they just don't have any more talk left in them. Resist the temptation to make them feel just a teensy bit bad about being such a wet mop, because they are already berating themselves like crazy and growing mildly depressed about their inability to muster up the required energy.

When they are on top of the world, their dreamy story-telling and eccentricities have them charming everybody in the room. Despite their ancient countenance, they are surprisingly easy to kid and they often fall prey to other people's more wicked sense of humour. In the dictionary, the word gullible should be illustrated with a little fish.

Pisces are much better in one-on-one situations when their thoughtful and intuitive responses are able to be honed in one direction. They tell a whimsy story, often picking out the most unusual details to colour their tale to very good effect.

You can sometimes get the impression that your Pisces friend is lasting out the conversation with you out of a sense of obligation and this can be for two reasons.

The first is because Pisces often doesn't know how to end an interaction, even when they really should be leaving soon/putting on the dinner/getting back to work. They will often just sound more and more distracted and strained until you put them out of their misery and declare that you really should be off now.

The other is much more spiritual and more to do with their life journey than you. Pisces just tend to feel like a) they have tonnes more time on their hands than the rest of us (after all, this is at least their twelfth time around on the planet) and b) there is nothing much that hasn't been said before and nothing that you have to say will have a lot of impact on them or the world. This can manifest itself into an amused, if not just a wee bit smug, smile that speaks volumes. It says, 'Come now little whippersnapper, why worry now? It will happen one day, if not in this lifetime, then the next.'

They can throw a surprisingly good party though, because it gives them the inflexibility of a fixed deadline to work to. Pisces are notorious procrastinators and will find any little loophole to exploit when trying to push out a time-line, but a party date is much more difficult to chop and change. Pisces will usually rise to this challenge and put in the effort to make their preparations orderly and logical, as opposed to their usual preparatory style, which is distracted and dithering. Their fertile imagination makes sure the affair will be a little different from the norm and that every-one will be talking about the night for weeks to come.

How to Woo Your Pisces

Pisces women are old-fashioned ladies at heart, and don't let them tell you any different. The odd one will attempt to put up the modern woman front, but she will turn to mush if you run around and open the car door for her. Treat her like she is the most precious and delicate flower you ever came across, and she will melt right there in front of you.

They will probably be nervous, so you might have to take the reins of the conversation for the first half-hour or so (this is not always true, some Pisces come into their own in romance and will be quite aggressive in their flirt-ing). A night at the theatre or the ballet and they will be in their element. A nice idea for a daytime date is 'high tea' at a posh hotel. It's all marvellously civilised and a lot of fun. Pisces love play-acting at being posh.

Once things get a little more intimate, make any excuse to give her a foot massage. Pisceans completely bliss out as soon as you touch their feet.

Gifts for Your Pisces

Because Pisces sometimes have to be forced into doing things for themselves, and are also notorious for ignoring their health, consider a voucher for a relaxation massage or a paid-up course in tai chi.

If your Pisces is the self-destructive type, stay away from presents of alcohol, but a great fantasy novel or a fantasy computer game will thrill them. Don't expect to see them for the next couple of days, though.

Pisces are soppy old sentimentalists for the most part, so frame a wedding photo of their grandparents or their parents or arrange a slide night for them – really rummage around in the box for some unusual old slides. Set the atmosphere with some well-chosen music. They will be misty-eyed and reaching for the tissues by the end of it.

If you have been away for some time and have received letters from them (Pisceans are fantastic letter writers, but terrible emailers), make them dinner and read through the letters over a bottle of red wine. This is a blue-ribbon winner with the nostalgic Pisces.

They like trinkets and old-fashioned things. Piscean women retain their girly quality throughout their lives. A music box or a china doll or teddy bear with the scent of eras past always goes down well.

Anything to encourage the considerable creative talents of Pisces is great, but getting them to sit down to do it in between all their commitments to other people is another thing. This is why booking them into a course like painting is for their own good, as they will have to go and enjoy it because they are doing it for you! They also particularly like gifts associated with water.

OTHER COMPATIBILITIES

ARIES/ARIES

Temper tantrums erupt into major wars. Only one party can win and you both hate defeat. Hot and fiery.

ARIES/TAURUS

Taureans make money. Aries spend it, so the Bull toils diligently without seeing the fruits of her labour. Compromise is a must.

ARIES/CANCER

The Crab is far too sensitive and slow for Aries' tempestuous nature. Aries has difficulty listening to the Crab's negativity. Tolerance is the key.

ARIES/LEO

Exhilaration plus. Sharing the same likes and dislikes, you lead a charmed life, searching out excitement, love, laughs and fun.

ARIES/VIRGO

Aries' impulsiveness is just too much and Virgo's practical, critical nature will drive Aries to drink. Barely patient sighs will abound.

ARIES/LIBRA

Aries can't tell his claret from his beaujolais, and lacks sophistication. Libra is too lazy for speedy Aries. Fun while it lasts.

ARIES/SCORPIO

A hot and heavy union, but too hot to handle for the carefree Aries as the possessive Scorpio will give you a short leash.

ARIES/SAGITTARIUS

You are both fun-loving people and oblivious to the faults in each other that might drive other people loopy. Laughter and love.

ARIES/CAPRICORN

Aries can spend it as fast as the Goat can make it, which

drives the bean-counting Capricorn to despair. Compromise.

ARIES/AQUARIUS

Great conversation and a good game of chess; however, this time Aries is the one guessing. Who will call who, and when? Interesting.

ARIES/PISCES

The Fish will find Aries intellectualising superficial and Aries will find Pisces' emotional games exhausting.

TAURUS/TAURUS

Same-sign relationships are always trying. However, you make a welcoming home and will put on scrumptious dinner parties.

TAURUS/CANCER

Pure bliss! Cancer makes a good home and gives physical affection, which is all Taurus wants. Sensual heaven on earth. A lovely match.

TAURUS/LEO

Great sex appeal, magnanimous Leo will shower Taurus with the finer things in life. Longevity, stability and loyalty. Worth a red-hot go.

TAURUS/VIRGO

An earthy love tryst. The common desire for material wealth and security will see you through.

TAURUS/LIBRA

Venus rules both these signs and gives their pairing harmony. Pots of money required to appease their desire for luxury.

TAURUS/SCORPIO

Taurus must appear to be wholly and solely committed at all times. In the long run, this can wear thin, even for the diligent Bull.

TAURUS/SAGITTARIUS

Two very different life philosophies. Both must agree that no way is the better way, and to love each other for it.

TAURUS/CAPRICORN

Capricorn will be aloof at first, but the warm rays of Venus will soon melt the exterior of caution in the Goat.

TAURUS/AQUARIUS

If you seem like you are from opposite sides of the planet, that is because you are. A similar sense of humour may see you through.

TAURUS/PISCES

Taurus' practicality can comfort the emotional Pisces. Pisces allows earth-bound Taurus to dream a little. Usually a joy.

CANCER/CANCER

Sensual bedmates, both are too sensitive, too demanding and in need of an enormous amount of reassurance.

CANCER/LEO

Cancer might shy from Leo's exuberance, but like the moon reflects the sun, you can both feed each other's good qualities.

CANCER/VIRGO

Cancer will warm up Virgo, and steady Virgo helps balance variable Cancer. Cancer's dependency complements Virgo's protective side.

CANCER/LIBRA

Cancer seeks emotional partnering, Libra seeks intellectual communion. Sexual rapport is not affectionate enough for Cancer.

CANCER/SCORPIO

Both value emotional commitment and Cancer's sensuality ignites Scorpio's passion. Together they build a love cocoon with intimacy, intensity and depth.

CANCER/SAGITTARIUS

Cancer's imagination complements Sagittarius' worldly knowledge, but better friends than lovers. Cancer needs reassurance, which is a Sagittarius blindspot.

CANCER/CAPRICORN

Cancer plays sensitive flower to Capricorn's domineering protector. Adjustments have to be made, but worth the effort.

CANCER/AQUARIUS

Cancer needs security; Aquarius is a lone wolf who, if trapped, will gobble up Cancer's warm, responsive nature. Not a great idea.

CANCER/PISCES

Pisces love protective Cancer, Cancer loves having someone to love, especially the emotionally responsive Pisces. A nurturing match.

LEO/LEO

Cooperation. Ah, yes, not something that comes easily to either of you. Like two king lions in a pride, you can expect to butt heads a little.

LEO/VIRGO

Leo loves Virgo's sexy coolness, Virgo loves Leo's warmth;

Virgo plays handmaiden to Leo's success, enjoying the glamour from behind the logbooks.

LEO/LIBRA

These two will enjoy fabulous sex romps, but when it finally gets down to the nitty-gritty of commitment, there may be some problems.

LEO/SCORPIO

A clash of wills. Mutual attraction to strength of character adds to the conquest, but once caught that proud, stubborn streak gets up your left nostril.

LEO/SAGITTARIUS

Sagittarius will keep introducing new ideas and experiences to keep Leo from getting into a rut. Sagittarius adds the humour and Leo adds the panache. A good match.

LEO/CAPRICORN

Leo's gaudy temperament clashes with Capricorn's refined colour scheme. Leos are bombastic when it comes to intellectual detail, which irritates Capricorn.

LEO/AQUARIUS

Leo loves the world and Aquarius loves humanity. Leo loves a good surprise and Aquarius can provide. Fun.

LEO/PISCES

Leo will never have to vie for the spotlight with Pisces, but Leo can trample Pisces' feelings. Leo finds Pisces too clingy and stifling.

VIRGO/VIRGO

The constant self-criticism of the Virgo mind doubled. Try not to be too hard on each other. Happiness in the details.

VIRGO/LIBRA

Virgo views Libra as wishy-washy, Libra views Virgo as prim. As a learning relationship your different natures can complement each other.

VIRGO/SCORPIO

Scorpio strides fearlessly, Virgo treads carefully; Virgo doesn't like to get his hands dirty, while Scorpio is more primitive. Harmonising.

VIRGO/SAGITTARIUS

Sagittarius takes care of the forest, Virgo straightens every bough and sweeps away the pesky leaves. The joy is in communicating.

VIRGO/CAPRICORN

Marvellously productive, Capricorn provides the strategy and Virgo the talent. Guard against predictability.

VIRGO/AQUARIUS

Good mental rapport, Virgo focuses on details, while Aquarius takes a global view. May be too cool to get off the ground.

VIRGO/PISCES

Ambiguity is the bane of Virgo's existence, but Pisces will absorb lots of contradictory ideas. Pisces is poetry to Virgo's facts. Sensitivity will unite.

LIBRA/LIBRA

For both of you, your feelings seem real when you share the experience. You invest enormous energy into personal relationships. Harmony and balance.

LIBRA/SCORPIO

Scorpio has an urge to merge, Libra likes to keep a sense of proportion. An interesting match.

LIBRA/SAGITTARIUS

A party duo, outgoing and friendly, Sagittarius provides the grandiose ideas, Libra puts them into perspective.

LIBRA/CAPRICORN

Capricorn can keep Libra in the style to which she is accustomed, Libra can infuse some wine and laughter into Capricorn's orderly life.

LIBRA/AQUARIUS

Great mates with a lust for conversation. You both like things pretty breezy, Aquarius more so than Libra. To the happy couple.

LIBRA/PISCES

Affectionate, creative, artistic both, a romantic couple, but Pisces won't find emotional support in Libra and Libra won't find the luxury she craves.

SCORPIO/SCORPIO

Whoa baby, this is intense. Scorpios are all or nothing, so this must be all. Stormy fights and sizzling reunions typify your relationship.

SCORPIO/SAGITTARIUS

Sagittarius feels Scorpio is a dead weight, Scorpio (correctly) suspects Sagittarius doesn't care as much. Sagittarius doesn't have the capacity for Scorpio's depth of feeling.

SCORPIO/CAPRICORN

Naturally suspicious, neither of you is flippant about affection. There is no froth and bubble here – but you don't want that anyway.

SCORPIO/AQUARIUS

Scorpio needs to possess the person and Aquarius wants to own the world, but these two desires are not mutually exclusive. A taste for the unusual.

SCORPIO/PISCES

Scorpio's jealousy makes Pisces feel loved and Pisces' dependency is Scorpio's strength. Communication is on a sensual, unspoken level. Heaven on earth.

SAGITTARIUS/SAGITTARIUS

Unparalleled lust for life, the camaraderie between you is infectious. Guard against superficiality, things might fizzle into just good friends

SAGITTARIUS/CAPRICORN

Optimism and faith versus realism and doubt. Capricorn finds Sagittarius' plans amusing, Sagittarius finds that reaction just a little bit patronising. Worth it.

SAGITTARIUS/AQUARIUS

Friendly but somewhat detached, this will worry neither of you. A fashionable partnering, you will always know what is up. Enjoyable and interesting.

SAGITTARIUS/PISCES

Lusty, but Pisces is a dreamer, not a doer, which will frustrate Sagittarius no end. Sagittarius' sharp tongue will puncture Pisces' dream bubble.

CAPRICORN/CAPRICORN

Stability and love in abundance but light and laughter could be lacking, so have kids, the more the merrier. A long and fruitful love.

CAPRICORN/AQUARIUS

Capricorn brings tenacity and reliability. Aquarius brings ingenuity and sensitivity to current trends. Some warmth and sexual spark makes an interesting match.

CAPRICORN/PISCES

Like a puzzle, these two personalities fill in the weaknesses of the other. Capricorn makes the decisions, Pisces brings the romance. One-plus-one unites.

AQUARIUS/AQUARIUS

Friends or lovers – can lovers still be friends? Of course! You both cry. What happens when lovers are only friends? Hmmm. Softness required.

AQUARIUS/PISCES

Sexually, this is fun, but sex is never enough to keep Aquarius interested. Pisces will struggle to communicate subtle emotional undertones. Not a happy story.

PISCES/PISCES

Eventually you are both going to have to open the shutters and face the real world. One of you must pay the bills – which one is it going to be?